City and Islington Sixth Form College
The Angel 283-309 Goswell Road
London EC1V 7LA
020 7520 0652

CITY AND ISLINGTON
COLLEGE

This book is due for return on or before the date last stamped below.
You may renew by telephone. Please quote the Barcode No.
May not be renewed if required by another reader.

Fine: 10p per day

7129

LORNA OWENS

EVERYDAY GRACE, EVERYDAY MIRACLE:
LIVING THE LIFE YOU WERE BORN TO LIVE

Blessings Press Miami

Blessings Press
Miami, Florida

Telephone 305-573-8423
www.lornaowens.com

Library of Congress Cataloging-in-Publication Data

Owens, Lorna: Everyday Grace Everyday Miracle: Living
the Life You were Born To Live /by Lorna Owens

p.cm
1. Inspiration 1. Title

ISBN-13: 978-0-9790778-0-7
ISBN-10: 0-9790778-0-X
Library of Congress Control Number: 2006910359

Book Design : Stuart Lyle

Printed in The United States of America

5 1 4 9 5 5 1

In Memory of my
father Clifford Vernon
and Dedicated to my
mother Zettie Vernon

CONTRIBUTING AUTHORS

Char McCargo Bah

Sharon Beth Brani

Kathy Bruins

Dinorah Blackman

Johnese Burtram

Grace Boneschansker

Reverend Dr. Lori Cardona

Lucy Cain

Lisa Cohen

Angalette Dye

Minister Mary Edwards

Karen Elengikal

Peggy Frezon

Anne Fitz Henry

Pam Hirson

Mary Haskett

Eve Eschner Hogan

Dahlia Walker Huntington

Susan Karas

Karen Reno Knapp

Chef Stefano LaCava

Nancy Lucas

Catherine Madera

Lakisha McClendon

Christine Miles

Valora Otis

Diane Pitts

S. Brenton Rolle

Melissa Annette Santiago

Pachent Gordon –Smythe

Chaya Srivatsa

Lynne Cooper Sitton

Vera Thomas

Terri Tiffany

Tonie –Beth Vernon

Estella Washington

Karen Ward

Lora Woodhall

Dallas Nicole Woodburn

Suzanne Windon

Barbara Williams

Debbie Willows

Nicole Wild

Amy Wiley

Thank you

CONTENTS

FORWARD

WE ALL TELL STORIES about what we've endured as a way to celebrate our triumph over adversity, and to encourage each other to believe in better days. We know, too, that sharing our delight in the wonderful things that happen to us lifts our own hearts and inspires others. The stories you will read in this book have been contributed by men and women from all over the world. I share them for the purpose of connecting us all to the truth that every day we experience grace and miracles. We need only to look closely and listen carefully to see the hand of God and hear the voice of God in our lives. When we learn to tune into the presence of God, our hearts are open and our lives are full of joy.

Imagine, as you read, that you are joining with the many thousands of others who are reading this book as well. Know that we are gathered together in this shared experience of passing on stories in our own voice. I hope this book will encourage you to share your stories of grace and miracles in ever-widening circles, and that perhaps you will pass along the stories in this book to support someone else.

Engage With God

LET ME BEGIN with my own story. My name is Lorna Owens. I was born in a little village called Mandeville on the beautiful island of Jamaica, which is set like a jewel in the Caribbean Sea. My mother was twenty-eight and unmarried when I was born. She struggled to raise me on her own until I was twelve, and then she met and married an incredibly loving man. My stepfather was the only father I have known and he was truly wonderful.

My journey to wholeness started seven years ago, as I sat overwhelmed with sorrow at my father's funeral. He had died suddenly of a stroke and I had returned to Jamaica from my home in Miami to gather with family, friends, and people from the village. As we all crowded into the small church, I was filled with sadness and with pride. The sadness that touched my soul came from having to burying my father. I also felt proud of him because he had lived so well. My father had done for others all his life with compassion and consistency. His life had made a difference and he had experienced true fulfillment.

As I heard the minister's description of my father's life, I reflected on my own and let the scenes from each decade pass before my eyes. I didn't like the totality of what I saw. I had worked very hard and had succeeded in reaching my educational and professional goals, but I heard a voice inside me ask, *What have you done for others?* As I searched my soul for the answer, I listened carefully again to what people were saying about my father.

He had given money to couples to help them get married, and he visited people he knew were sick to provide money for the doctor. He even had helped families bury their dead. In a funeral full of song and story, my father's life was celebrated as having been full and complete. I knew that, if I died soon, my life would not be as complete. At that moment, I decided I wanted to be like my father. I decided I would change and would do so immediately. I would live filled with joy. I would find work that fulfilled me. And most of all, I would do things for others that would have a lasting impact.

I had already had two full careers by this time. I had completed my education and worked as a nurse and midwife. I had learned a great deal from that experience, but the work didn't feel the most like who I truly was. I was being of some use to people, but the job didn't connect me to them in quite the right way. Then, I had shifted to law, graduating from law school and working as a prosecutor with the state attorney's office in Miami under former Attorney General Janet Reno. After that, I established my own practice in criminal and entertainment law and was doing well financially, but again, something wasn't right. I did not have any energy and I found it very hard to get out of bed in the morning. No matter how much sleep I got, I was always tired. It wasn't that I was working too hard – I loved hard work – something else was the cause of my fatigue. I ruled out medical problems to make sure I wasn't physically ill. But it wasn't until my father's funeral that I understood it was my soul and heart that were sick. I needed to change my life in big ways.

When I returned to Miami, I made a fundamental mistake. I didn't slow down to ask God to guide my decisions. I had listened to the voice that asked, What have you done for others? But I hadn't gotten quiet and asked God, *What do you think I should do*? At that time in my life, I felt so competent and sure of what I could accomplish on my own that it hadn't occurred to me to engage with God. I didn't know that I simply needed to listen patiently for the answer.

Moment-to-Moment God

Sometimes we feel and act as if God is only a special-occasion God. We miss so much when we hold this view. I now understand that having a relationship with God is a moment-to-moment experience and not a rare one. God is interested in every detail of our lives. God knows when even a sparrow falls. He knows our pain and we can call on Him in our dark times. But He also knows when every sparrow soars and sings, and God wants us to be in touch when we're planning and dreaming and working to make new things happen in our lives.

God is not out there somewhere far away to be called upon only rarely, but is right beside us all the time. As soon as we pull God close to us, the relationship moves from our head to our heart and our life changes from the inside. When we shift to a close relationship with God we can see miracles happen every day and not only in response to a call of desperation.

In the years that led up to this change in my life, I had experienced a turbulent relationship with God. I had a bad habit of only praying in desperation. I didn't understand that my relationship with Him could be easy, pleasant and full of love and trust. I hadn't yet learned that I could share my intimate daily thoughts with God. As it happened, I would learn this lesson the hard way.

When I returned from Jamaica, I promptly closed my law offices and opened a record company called Positive Vibe Music. I thought I could handle these changes on my own and so, without God's involvement, I jumped in with both feet. I believed in my abilities and I knew I had creativity that could be tapped in this new venture. So, I strapped myself into a roller-coaster ride that went too fast to stop and was too much out of control. I would be totally broke and very near homelessness before the ride ended. But before things got much worse, they seemed to be pretty good for a time.

Shortly after I opened the record company, I was approached with the opportunity to launch a new reggae artist. He was from Jamaica, his music was fantastic, and I created a launch for him that I was told was the best Miami Beach had ever seen. The Miami Ballet choreographed a piece for the event. There were trips to Chicago and New York to launch in those markets as well. And I lined up media interviews and performances. I was good at the work and enjoyed it very much. I touched into a part of me that had been dormant since I had attended the Jamaica School of Speech and Drama. I was good at turning a creative vision into reality.

At this time, I had also met an incredible Jamaican gospel artist named Joy White. She was a star. She had the individuality and power of artists like Tracy Chapman and Phoebe Snow. I recorded and released a double single for her, and it rocketed to number one in Jamaica and number ten on the gospel charts in the United States. It was a wonderful breakthrough. I had a number-one artist! I invested all my money in the record company and in her future. It was a risky business because I had to invest up front in all of the expenses we incurred to record and promote our albums. I had to advance plane fares, meals, clothing, lodging, and even had to pay for performances and venues for my artists. I had closed my law offices and so no new income was coming in. I had dismantled the entire infrastructure that supported my income and the record company had to work or I'd lose everything.

But then, my key artist got ill, stayed ill for a very long time and my world came crumbling down. I lost all my money and was on the brink of homelessness as I tried to stay afloat. Only now that I was a half-step away from disaster, did I finally talk to God. *You will have your season of blessing*, I heard His voice say. "It had better happen real soon!" I replied.

I do not know if you understand this feeling, but I felt like I had been taken up to the mountain top, had looked over and seen the promised land, then was brought back to earth to do the work. I had to get up and do the work. The voice said that if I did the work, I would have great success. I share this to encourage you to work hard and hold on. Never ever ever quit.

God is a God of second chances and in order to help you change He may need to deconstruct your life so that it can be remade in His glory. He will help you reconstruct your life. If you are in a situation like I was and you are wondering how you got yourself in the mess you're in, do not lose faith. You will make it through. It was only when I ventured into my darkest night of the soul that I was forced to turn my life over to God. I use the word "forced" because even on the verge of bankruptcy and utter defeat, I still had a very health ego and believed I could figure out *something* to make things work out all right. I just didn't get it.

Then, one day it dawned on me at long last that I did not have the wherewithal emotionally, physically, or financially to pull myself out of this one. I realized I had better start depending on God for help and guidance. I had to read the bible, pray and get myself grounded. This necessity hit me like a ton of bricks, and I was surprised I hadn't realized this before. No wonder my life was such a mess.

The Bible is food, soul food. It nourishes the soul just as the food we eat nourishes our bodies. Once I discovered this truth, I followed the realization with action. I kicked myself into gear swiftly and worked fiercely at my new commitment because I did not want to fall into the abyss. I had no other choice. All other avenues of escape were cut off and there was only one door through which I could pass. Somehow, I got my ego got out of the way and walked through the door God had opened for me, but I did so kicking and screaming. Then, to my amazement, I walked into a brand-new day. And the days since then have truly been the best days of my life.

I had filed for bankruptcy, almost lost my home, and a loan officer had spoken to me like I was the scum of the earth. Some of my friends lost the respect they had for me. Others friends simply stopped calling. But God had designed a plan for my life far bigger and grander than I could have designed for myself and I had to trust and move forward to help make it happen.

A Holy Stop

We've all experienced ups and downs in life. Sometimes there are small descents and rises, and at other times the downs take us down so deep we're not sure we'll ever see the light again, and the highs lift us up so high we suddenly see who we truly are and how we were meant to live. Sometimes, in the midst of these ups and downs we reach a crossroads and face critical choices but have no idea what is happening to us, or where to go or what to do. When nothing seems to be working and confusion closes in around us, that's an opportunity I call a holy stop.

When you really have no idea what's becoming of your life, it is possible that you are being called to do real work – kingdom work – and the Holy Spirit is making things really simple for you. He offers us only a single door through which we can pass. When we have no other choices, it is a perfect time to wait on God. The wonderful blessing is that the Holy Spirit is at least pointing us in the right direction. Be grateful and know you will be directed toward something truly meaningful – your purpose. When that happens, there is no need to panic. It simply means that God understands that you are ready for a bigger assignment. Relax and give in to the guidance of the Holy Spirit. Simply rest on your relationship with God. Pray, read the Bible, and your life – a truer and more meaningful life – will return to you.

Let go and let God we hear in church time after time. And in each of our lives comes the moment when that is precisely what we are called to do. I remember one incident as if it were yesterday. It was 10:00 p.m. on a Sunday night. I had just said my prayers and blown out the candles I use to help set the tone for prayer. The incense was no longer burning in its holder and I had turned off the music I had been listening to – Schubert's Symphony No. 5 in B Flat Major and I felt very peaceful. I was rearranging my white fluffy pillows, preparing to sleep, when suddenly a voice told me to get up, go to my computer, and enter my name in a search engine on the Internet.

I got out of bed and uneasily followed the instruction. The first entry that came up – on Dade County's official website – was a notice that my home would be sold in five days on the Court House steps. At first I felt nothing and did nothing; I was totally numb. But as the blood returned to my extremities, I started feeling hot, then cold, then hot again, and I was sure I was going to pass out. "Breathe," I kept telling myself, "breathe."

I called my friend Fred, a mortgage broker. I told him I urgently needed him to find me money – any money – and fast. Strangely, I was not panicked. I had a Godly knowing that everything was going to be all right. Any successful survivor will tell you the worst thing you can do in a life-threatening situation is to panic. If you panic, you will die. On that night, God kept me from panicking. He led me to my computer, then to my friend Fred, who, in turn, introduced me to a colleague, who was able to guarantee me the funds I desperately needed and in less than five days.

It was the grace and the mercy of God that sent me to my computer that night. It was the grace of God that made me pay attention, and, as a result, I was able to save my home. But more than that, that night set me on the path I am now on. It is a path of total surrender to God. My experience of the Holy Stop that night allows me to be fully confident when I tell you it does not matter where you are in your life. You can, and you will, survive by the grace and mercy of God. You can be victorious, you can have a life rich with meaning, and you can discover your true purpose in this crazy mixed-up world. Out of something potentially horrible came the greatest breakthrough of my life, and a similar breakthrough is waiting for you.

Remembering

The other day I was running late for a meeting and, as happens a lot, a word popped into my head. This time, it was the word "remember." At first I didn't get it. Then, it hit me like a bolt of lightening. "Remember the goodness of God," the voice continued to say. "It is hard to be filled with fear and doubt if you remember." Can you imagine how one simple word can bring such blessings into your life? It can. Make the word "remember" part of your daily practice. Remember the place God delivered you from. Remember how God opened a new door for you when you felt there was no chance for renewal. Remember how God saw to it that you were in the right place at the right time. Simply remember. It is one of the very best ways to empower your life.

If we remembered more, we would quit complaining. I doubt God ever gets angry, but if he does, surely nothing would make God angrier than those times when we forget His goodness and mercy and start complaining. I say that because I, too, do not practice remembering as I should at all times and I get very impatient.

I think of the story of Moses and the children of Israel and how God parted the Red Sea so the children of Israel could cross into Egypt safely. Yet still they forgot His many blessings to them and started complaining that they should have stayed in Israel. It was forgetting that caused the Israelites to wander in the wilderness for forty years – there were consequences, it seems, for forgetting the goodness of God. And there are consequences for complaining. It is no wonder that when we forget we do not grow, no wonder when we complain we do not prosper.

In the end, I withdrew from the bankruptcy proceedings and I have never looked back. I paid everyone I owed, because for me at that time it was the right thing to do. All I needed was space in which to breathe and some time to find a second chance.

In the Palm of His Hand

It is also important for us to remember past victories. I remember a day when I had only one hundred dollars to my name, and I did not want to spend all of it when I went to the supermarket. So, I took only twenty dollars with me when I went out, and as I walked into the supermarket, a voice said, "Look down," and on the parking-lot pavement I found five dollars. I spent twenty three dollars and six cents on groceries and then, on my way home, I found another five-dollar bill. It was a day of victories, and anytime I feel downcast I try to remember it. I'm reminded again and again that God will provide for us no matter what might be happening around us.

Understand that if God has healed you before, he will come through again. If God has provided for you in the past, he will provide for you again. Use these moments of remembering in order to sustain your life and connect your heart with the goodness of God – this is one of the most powerful tools you have. And you can take that to the bank. I did.

Even if you are sure you have the answers – or perhaps *particularly* if you're sure – live your life asking God for answers. Ask God if this is the right relationship for you, the best job, the truest use of your talents and skills. Had I not gone through all my crises, I would not have the skills I now possess. I would not have tapped into my creativity in such meaningful ways. At one point in time I literally could not have imagined that I would be doing the work I do now, but now I cannot imagine doing anything else. And I believe everything I have gone through was critical preparation for the work I now do. Had I known beforehand what road I would have to travel to get where I am today, I would have quickly said, "Lorna Owens, reporting for duty, Lord." And when we meet in person, I'll look you in the eyes and tell you without an ounce of doubt that God is in control of my life now. God has me in the palm of His hand and I will never be afraid again.

I encourage you to remember two things: one is that is very possible for your life to take such a wrong detour that you feel you will never make it back to your proper path safely. I know; I came very close to having that happen. The second is to listen closely to the small voice of the Holy Spirit, calling you away from tragedy and back to safety. What is your own small voice telling you to do? It could be that it is time for you to start your own business, go back to school, add more spirituality or service to your life, or it could be time to walk away from that toxic relationship. I do not know. But all of us hear that small voice from time to time. Learn to listen to it. Learn to trust it and learn to follow it. I have learned to listen to God and act according to his guidance with regard to just about everything in my life. I mean everything. I do not disregard the whispers of the Holy Spirit, and because of that, I live with trust.

People often talk to me about "coincidences" that happen in their lives. I don't believe in coincidences, I believe that God is the giver of all good things and that certain patterns tend to emerge as we move toward God. There are no coincidences, only God's wide hand of protection. It is no coincidence that you are reading this book on this particular day. Let us give God praise for *everything* that happens in our lives, including the "coincidences" that have lead you to this book and a connection to those who will share their stories with you and those with whom you will share your stories in turn.

Quiet Time
: Chapter Two

WE LIVE IN A FAST-PACED WORLD where we often spend more than we earn trying to feel good, look young, and impress others. We are constantly scanning for something new and different, and are often far too busy. We are in debt to the hilt, we are stressed, we are anxious, and, sadly, we are out of touch with our deeper nature and with God. We badly need moments of calm in our lives, but instead we stay "productive" by working long hours, running errands, e-mailing, shopping, and cleaning. When our work is done, we tend to stay distracted by watching television, surfing the Internet, and still keeping up a frantic pace even when we have an opportunity to slow down.

Sometimes, we schedule quiet time, but instead of tuning into the stillness, we are lost in a jumble of thoughts and become more anxious as a result. If we load up our precious free time with pursuits that keep us totally occupied, we loose a sacred opportunity. And, ironically, we can even overdo our desire to improve our lives by spending our free time reading books and attending workshops and retreats to learn how to have a better life, and then neglect to take the time necessary to integrate what we have learned in stillness and in quiet. I say, let's get out of our own way. Let's get out of our own heads and give ourselves some quality quiet time.

From Frantic to Godly Quiet

A friend of mine recently complained that her brain hurt. I asked for clarification. Did she have a headache? She responded that her brain hurt because it felt overloaded with so much going on at work, so much to do at home trying to be the perfect wife and mother, and then trying to take care of herself as well. When she told me what she did in just one day I had to admit that my brain hurt just hearing her tick off the long list. It's hard to make a living, to try and raise a Godly family, and to be a super man or woman. And our lives are often incredibly stressful.

WE TEND TO EXPERIENCE STRESS FROM FOUR BASIC SOURCES:

1. *The Environment.* The noise, pollution, and visual over-stimulation that is so common in our surroundings and can overwhelm us.

2. *Social stressors.* Outside forces such as deadlines, financial pressures, long hours on the job, and the demands of friends and family can keep our stress levels at the boiling point.

3. *Physiological stress.* Chronic health conditions, biological stresses like menopause in women, serious illness, aging, and a lack of exercise and weight gain can significantly increase stress.

4. *Our thoughts.* The brain interprets our emotional distress and turns on our body's emergency responses. If we are constantly in a flight or fight mode, we overtax our ability to cope. How we interpret and label our experience and how optimistic we feel about the future can either relax us or stress us even more.

Hans Selye, one of the first people to conduct major research on stress, found that any problem, real or imagined, can cause a biological response. When a potential stressor is identified by your brain, the cerebral cortex sends an alarm to the hypothalamus. That, in turn, stimulates the sympathetic nervous system to make a series of changes in your body. Your heart races. You start breathing faster. Your hands and feet get cold as blood is directed away from your extremities and digestive system and into the larger muscles that help you fight or flee.

Problems arise when the fight or flight response continues to be stimulated – as it does under the conditions of chronic stress. Your adrenal glands secrete corticoids (adrenaline or epinephrine and norephidrine), which inhibit digestion, reproduction, growth, tissue repair, and the response of your immune system.

Fortunately, the same mechanism that turns on the stress response can also turn it off. This is called the relaxation response. As soon as you decide a situation is no longer stressful, your brain stops sending panicked messages to your nervous system. Three minutes after you send the signal to shut off the threat, your brain stops sending those urgent messages to your nervous system and the fight or flight response burns off, allowing your metabolism, heart and breathing rate, muscle tension, and blood pressure to return to normal.

Knowing that we are so much better off quieting our stress, what can we do when faced with more tasks than we can ever really accomplish in a day? I think the place to start is by praying for guidance about our true priorities and deciding what to do based on our inner guidance. The most powerful tool we have in dialing down the stress of our lives is to give ourselves the gift of Godly quiet.

This kind of quiet means more than the absence of noise and distraction. This kind of quiet is about doing nothing, resting deeply, and letting God fill the space in our body and soul.

Be Still and Know That I Am God

The stresses of our lives can take us to some dark places and it can seem as if we are walking alone, but when we rest, we go into the silence and gather our strength. It is in this holy silence that we ask for and accept God's help. Even though God is always there for us, He does not force that help upon us. We have the opportunity to exercise our free will and invite that assistance. Then we learn to trust God's heart, even when we cannot see His hand.

When I speak of Godly quite time, I mean something different from prayer time. For me prayer is a time to give thanks and to ponder the word of God and ask for His guidance. The quiet time I'm referring to is the empty space we need in order to hear God speaking to us – once we're done talking ourselves. Here's one example to illustrate why I think quiet time is so important.

One day after I had prayed and meditated, I was sitting on my balcony overlooking the water and letting the quiet fill me. I had been crying out to God for help. I was financially broke, I was broken in spirit, and my body was exhausted. I did not know what to do. As I waited in the quiet, I heard God say to me, "And the women gather." I did not know the phrase, but found it comforting. I jotted the words down in my journal with the note that perhaps one day I would write a book with the title *And The Women Gather.*

At another time a couple of years later I heard the guidance, *The time is right.* I inquired, *For what?* And again the phrase *and the women gather,* came into my consciousness. I said, *I have not begun to write that book yet.* But the voice said, *it is an evening of empowerment by women for women.*

That was five years ago, and that evening event has now evolved into an award-winning Literary Jazz Brunch that includes the inspiring words of best-selling authors from around the world. Five hundred women come. We have a great time and are motivated to live well. We laugh, we cry, we listen to jazz, we have a soul-nourishing and delicious brunch, and then we go home to live our lives with renewed enthusiasm until we return to be together again on the third Saturday of every March.

This event supports a nonprofit effort I began that trains women who are incarcerated to make better choices and inspires them to improve their lives in dramatic ways. The ninety-day empowerment program I conduct with inmates has touched many lives, and I intend to implement it in other locations around the world. All of this soulful work and great fun came from simply sitting still in one moment and listening to what filled the silence.

These gifts and breakthroughs come through clearly in the silence of our quiet time. If you are open to experimenting with this concept, start now with just five minutes of silence. It's hard to spend longer until you've developed the habit, but I've found that as soon as people get accustomed to taking five minutes every day to listen to God they can comfortably extend the time. It is important not to rush or force these few moments. Remember, this is your God time – all you have to do is to be open to what the Holy Spirit wants to share with you.

The Lilies Of The Field

As I write these words I am sitting at an open-air restaurant at the Ritz Carlton hotel in Jamaica. Only five years ago, I was looking under my couch cushions for change to buy groceries, and today I'm listening to a steel band playing softly in the background and enjoying a cup of tea and a gentle breeze. My Jamaican waiter tells me his name but I don't quite catch it. When I ask him to repeat his name, he smiles and tells me I can call him Lemon Pie. I laugh and thank him for the gift of who he is. I watch as he engages with the other guests, having fun, and clearly loving his job. The goodness and peace of my surroundings and the happiness of those around me lifts my soul with joy. I take one of my quiet moments right there in front of everyone. I'm the woman with the blissed-out smile who closes her eyes and then gazes at the sky in silence. I enjoy the minutes that pass. I listen to God in the quiet.

Worry not about tomorrow and what you should eat or drink, and consider the lilies of the field the scripture tells us. If God provides for the birds and the flowers of the earth, how much more does He provide us? These days I find myself taking one precious day at time. I slow down enough to notice my brothers and sisters and to fully experience the feeling of grateful for the abundance that surrounds us all.

I have been in Jamaica for four glorious days. I am here to make arrangements for a new retreat called Women Travel First Class. I am excited, but I also feel trepidation. I know it is a big commitment of time and money. Yet I am at that place in my life where I need to take the next step. As I sit, I quiet my thoughts so that I can hear from God. I am seeking guidance about where to take this retreat. I want to have a good feel for who will come and what God has in store for the women who will take part in the event. I want to know how I can support the event in all the right ways. I feel I have been instructed and guided in this direction and I do not want my ego or fear to mess it up.

In the past, I've experienced many kinds of success and failure and these experiences have taught me that God has a plan for my life that is better than my plan. I prefer to surrender to doing what God wants me to do and trust that if I serve Him, the right things will happen at the right time.

In the silence, I feel a sense of encouragement and peace that tells me things are unfolding as they should. Later, I enjoy a massage that grounds the feeling of peace in my body. When I can treat myself to a massage I do, and when I can't, I put my arms around myself and give myself the best massage I can to help take the stress out of my body and to feel at peace.

We need to attend to our body and spirit in the ways that serve who we are. I find something powerfully restorative in fragrant oils, incense, music, and a beautiful candle after a long soak with a good bath salt. I call it scent and sound therapy, and I know that for me it helps produce the alpha waves that take me into a truly relaxed state. Do you know what soothes your soul? Do you know how and where you can create regular quiet time? Is it after reading a good book in front of a warm fire? Can you sit with a nice cup of tea, eat just the right thing, and then relax and pray and listen to the quiet? We all can learn to take better care of ourselves without spending money or leaving home, and our spirits will celebrate the chance to relax.

I am not standing in your shoes, so I do not know how or where you can create quiet time. I do know it is vital to indulge our senses and create a sacred space where we can relax and have time with God. I know a woman who gets up at five in the morning to pray and enjoy some quiet in her closet wrapped in a soft blanket. It's the only time of day and the only place in her house she can find a quite spot to herself, and she does it with joy because it keeps her life in balance.

Here in Jamaica I look and see the explosion of color all around and know our world was built for us to enjoy. I encourage you to put this book down for a moment and look at your surroundings, go outside or look out a window. Note the beauty you find in the first thing you see, take in all of the details with kind eyes and feel gratitude for the world we share.

Nourishing the Soul

I believe God intends for us to pay attention to color and light, the sound of the waves crashing on the shore, the songs of birds, and the happy clatter of the city. We benefit from paying attention to the moment we are experiencing, and we nourish our souls when we take the time to do nothing but let ourselves and the world be. Everyone I know, including me, feels guilty confessing, "I didn't do anything." We feel we've been wasteful, that we haven't been productive. I'm working to retrain myself to answer the question, "What did you do?" with the answer, "I nourished my soul." Instead of saying, "Nothing."

We move so fast these days that sometimes we just need to catch up with ourselves. We need to recover, recuperate, and regroup and bask in the wonders of God. We need to take the time to shout praises. All this and more is given birth in the stillness.

Nourishing the soul is much simpler than we might realize, and it has nothing to do with money. Don't put off quiet time or nourishing yourself by thinking that if you had the money you'd take a vacation to somewhere exotic and special. Beauty and peace can be found everywhere. I am writing in Jamaica, one of the most exotic and lovely places on earth. Yet, I see visitors and locals all around me who are running here and there not noticing the details of this place because they cannot sit still. I just spoke to a tourist who told me she was determined to pack every activity she could into her one week here. Her husband, she says, just wants to be as lazy as a llama. I encouraged her to soak up Jamaica like a plant taking in sunshine and water, and to experience her time here in whatever ways would be most nourishing to her soul.

Right now, look at your calendar and note four important words, *prayer time, quiet time.* They need to fit somewhere on your schedule and you need to have these times regularly. Everything else that needs to be done is less important. If your schedule is booked too full, find something on your list that isn't as essential as prayer time, quiet time and let it go. I decided I could find my time by being disciplined about not opening my e-mail first thing in the morning. I've learned to take prayer time, quiet time at the beginning of my day, before anything else demands my attention. I've learned to save things that aren't urgent for later; take my name off lists that generate busy work; make phone calls brief, warm, and to the point; turn off my cell phone; and to prioritize the tasks that fill the rest of my day. All of them are less important than the prayer time, quiet time that begins the day. One recent Sunday, I saw someone answer her cell phone in church. That seemed to confuse the point of what was most important in that particular moment.

Caring For The Body

I believe God wants us to engage fully in our lives and to appreciate and love our bodies. I think we're meant to face our days rested and full of the spirit. That's when we make good decisions, love well, and serve God. Take a break during the day when you feel tired. Stretch, take a deep cleansing breath, look up from your computer screen, take a brief walk, and meditate even for just a few minutes. Then go back to the task at hand and know that you will do much better and get more work done. Our body works in tandem with the work of our soul when we treat it with respect and care. Drinking extra coffee or a high energy drink to force ourselves to stay awake only provides a rush of false energy that will unfortunately lead to a crash. Not eating properly cheats us of the fuel we need to live well and with enthusiasm.

Being constantly busy and under stress can affect your body's defenses against infection. It affects your immune system and all the organs of your body. We must be very concerned about continuous stress. Stress can accumulate and pile up when the stress receptors are constantly turned on. If you haven't let go of it, the stress you hold in your body from years ago could still be affecting you now.

I didn't understand this at the time, but when I finally closed my law practice I was at the final stages of burnout. My body had begun shutting down in order to try to save me. Now I understand how important it is to cope with stress, and recognize when I need to ask for help, or simply stop. Stress is deadly, and it is insidious because we adjust and cope and are falsely proud when we continue to soldier on somehow. Don't become accustomed to the stress you're under. Tune into it and reduce it as a gift to yourself.

To learn about how your body holds onto stress, simply scan slowly from the bottom of your feet to the top of your head: do this right now to see where you are in this moment. Take a mental inventory of the areas where you feel tension and stress in your body. Now that you know where you feel the stress, focus your attention and touch to release it one area at a time. If you are like most people you might feel out of touch with your body at first. As you practice scanning and releasing tension, remind yourself that holding onto it hurts you, and that releasing it sets you free.

I also recommend keeping a stress-awareness journal in your calendar for a period of at least two weeks. Make a note of the times of day that are most stressful to you and what activity you are involved in when you feel the greatest stress. Be very specific so that you can identify negative patterns. For example: 8:00 a.m., just arrived at work and already feel tension in my neck and jaw. Your notes will teach you where the stresses are, when they occur, and how you can release them throughout the day.

Harness Your Imagination

You can significantly reduce your stress and improve your vision for your life with something enormously powerful and wonderfully personal to you – your imagination. While it's hard to will yourself into a relaxed state, you *can* imagine the feeling of relaxation spreading through your body and can visualize yourself in a safe and beautiful space. This act of imagination trips circuits in your brain that help you actually achieve the relaxation you first imagined.

Emile Coue, a French pharmacist, believed the power of imagination far exceeded that of the will. Coue asserted that all of our thoughts can become reality. Do you become what you think? What you obsessively worry about in a state of fear and stress can become your focus and feel real to you, unless you choose instead to dream of and work towards positive things, noting with optimism the good things that happen along the way. If you think sad thoughts, your sadness is reinforced and you become sad. When you look for the positive aspects of a situation you are likely to experience more hope.

There are some simple ways to make your visualization more effective. First, find a quiet place where you can be by yourself. Loosen your clothing, lie down, and close your eyes. Mentally scan your body to see if there is tension in any specific muscle. If you find tension, relax that muscle. Use a short and positive affirmation that reinforces your ability to relax in this moment. Use present tense and avoid negatives. Don't tell yourself "I am not tense," or "I must relax," but rather, say, "I am relaxing. I am relaxed. I feel at peace."

Imagine what your life would look like with greater balance and more of a connection with God. Imagine it fully and know that God wants that life for you and will attend to the challenges of helping you get there. Do you want more time with family and friends? More time to tend your garden? Work that is more fulfilling? Begin with your imagination and visualize what it will take to make those changes in your life. Imagine what you want to create as you relax and let go of stress. Then invite God to help make it possible.

The challenge is to choose with intention and care and follow through in ways that serve your larger goals in life. A friend of mine was experiencing so much stress at work that she decided to take a brief vacation to the south of France. She decided not to take her family; this would be time just for herself. She could afford the trip, so the cost wouldn't be a stress. I looked forward to hearing the details once she returned and assumed the experience would be soul-nurturing for her.

My friend had not visualized what she wanted from the experience. She hadn't gotten in touch with her body or soul about the trip. She had just booked a wonderful hotel and gone. She could have intentionally rested, wandered the streets with an open heart to see things in a new way in a new place, read a great book, enjoyed wonderful food, and spent time getting to know herself and engaging with God more fully. Sadly, that's not what happened. I had not heard from her a full week after the time she was due to return, so I called her. "How was your adventure?" I asked. "I hated it." she blurted.

My friend has been happily married for seventeen years and has two sweet children who are ages eleven and seven. She had never taken a vacation without her family. The moment she landed in France she decided she had made a big mistake taking the vacation without them. She imagined that it would have been perfect with them, and therefore would be a rotten experience alone. She spent all her time calling and e-mailing them and wishing she was having a different experience than the one she was having. I ached at the missed opportunity for her to have been more intentional about her journey, but I learned an important lesson as a result.

If you imagine that you cannot experience relaxation and joy unless you can afford to treat yourself to a trip to the French countryside, remember that you always take your reality with you, whatever it is, and however you choose to see it. You can find more joy in a long lunch at the French restaurant around the corner than my friend found in France, if you are present to the joys available in the moment.

Another friend of mine broke out his credit card and purchased a family cruise, then spent the weeks leading up to the trip experiencing terrible stress, worrying how he was going to pay for it. His wife saw his agony and the family sat down together to discuss the situation.

He got quiet and took the time to understand his stress and what was beneath it, and an answer emerged. He realized that it wasn't so much a question of not being able to afford the cruise, as it was feeling guilty about spending money on pleasure and relaxation. He had been raised to feel that fun was a waste and he simply couldn't feel good about spending hard-earned money on something frivolous. Together, he and his wife and children came up with a budget and a plan for affording the cruise without stress. Then they imagined the trip going well and visualized the closeness they would experience as a family and the memories they would make together. When it came time for the trip, they threw themselves into making the most soulful use of the experience. They had a great time, became closer, and nurtured themselves as individuals and as a family.

Sometimes that chatter in our heads can really do us in, until we let some stillness take care of it

Nourishing Your Spirit

The best advice I've ever received was that, above all else, I should feel passion for life as a way to praise the Creator who provided it. Nourish your spirit. When I say *spirit*, I mean whatever you know of as spirit in your own heart. In the German language, there are two words to represent distinctly different kinds of spirituality. Geistlich means spiritual matters reflecting a religious orientation, and Geistig refers to spiritual matters without ties to a specific religion. For some of us, organized religion is a good fit, for others a more personal spirituality is the key to our connection with God. At different times in our life, we might be drawn more to one kind of spirituality over another. Whatever your spiritual path, attend to your spiritual life by communing with God either in the presence of a congregation, or with the seagulls at the beach.

Recently, a woman named Kathy Bruins shared her story of spiritual renewal with me. Her experience is singular to her, but is also universal, since new doors opened as soon as Kathy invited God to help guide her life. Kathy was communing with God and walking her dog, when out of nowhere emerged the thought that she needed to lead a prayer ministry in her church. I'll let her tell you what happened next.

"Why am I thinking about this, God?" I wondered. I had never thought about the prayer ministry at all, but there the idea was and it was making my heart pound with excitement. "Lord, I don't know how to pray in any proper way!" What I meant was praying with structure and with eloquent words. God was probably thinking, "Just what are you doing right now?"

I thought I would walk a little more and perhaps the feeling would go away, but it hung on. "God, if this is of You, then You will have to make it very clear to me, because I'm not going to grab onto this idea by my-self." I finished the walk and returned home. I poured a cup of hazelnut coffee, enjoying the aroma as I walked to my desk. The phone rang as I sat down.

"Hi, Kathy. This is Lisa. I have a quick question about the drama coming up on Sunday." Lisa is one of the actors from the drama ministry I was leading. She is a very talented lady who has a great desire to serve the Lord. After talking a few minutes, she said, "Did you see that ad in the bulletin about the prayer leader position?"

I thought she would be the perfect person for the job. As I was about to encourage her to go for it, she said, "I really think you need to do it." I was speechless. Lisa finally asked, "Well, what do you think?" I shared with her my walking experience of less than fifteen minutes before. She laughed and said she knew God was guiding her.

I became the church's prayer leader. So, now what? I prayed that God would give me some direction, since He had gotten me into the situation. An image of a house came to mind, a literal house of prayer. I called my friend, Mike, who is great at building things and asked if he could create a model of a house of prayer with seven separate rooms. He came up with a drawing, which was perfect. After he built it, I thought it needed some color. A teenager who is on the drama team has many artistic gifts, so I asked her if she could design the colors and label the rooms of the house. She did a wonderful job!

I felt like Kevin Costner in *Field of Dreams*. If you build it, they will come. I displayed the House of Prayer visual along with a description of the prayer positions for each "room" or each team that would work in the House of Prayer. It was amazing how easily people came forward to be a part of the team. In a small church of only about two-hundred people, thirty-seven members of the congregation signed up. Seven of that number became the prayer facilitators who lead each team.

A conference was held in Grand Rapids called Prayer Fire. I signed up with a few other people to learn more about prayer and how we could make the most of our group. A workshop was being offered on healing prayer. Coming from a Reformed background, uneasiness about attending this workshop came over me, but at the same time, I felt drawn to attend it. The pastor leading the workshop explained the concept of healing so well that I felt no intimidation. I was excited to hear about his experiences with healing prayer. My heart again was grasped by the desire to pray.

At the end of the conference, the leaders of the workshops stood in a line. The host encouraged anyone in the audience who wanted prayer to come forward and stand before the next available person, who would then pray for them. There were hundreds of people who went up to receive prayer, but only about fifteen prayer leaders. I wasn't in a hurry, but I did think to myself, what would be the chance that I would end up with the healing prayer workshop leader?

As I got closer to the front, I saw that he was busy praying for someone. Then it was my turn. He looked at me, smiled, and waved me over. I told him I wasn't sure what I needed prayer for, but that I felt called to the healing prayer ministry. He anointed me with oil, prayed over me and I felt something that I hadn't felt before – a powerful feeling of energy. I couldn't move. He continued the prayer and whispered some words that I couldn't understand. I believe he was talking in tongues. The whisper sounded like a shout to my heart. I opened my eyes. I felt different, but not sure how. I thanked him and went back to my friends.

A few months passed, and after an evening service at our church, I asked another member of our drama team how he was doing. He explained that he had been suffering from sinus headaches all month. He was worn out from not being able to sleep because of the pain. A voice in my head said, "Go ahead, give it a try."

"Lord, I can't do that, they'll think I'm weird," my mind spoke back. "Don't worry. I will be with you." I nervously said to him, "John, I would like to pray for you here, if you don't mind."

He agreed. Other people were standing around, so I invited them to join us. At this point it just kept taking big leaps of faith.
We encircled John and I laid my hand on his shoulder. I invited everyone to pray who felt led to do so. It was a wonderful time of prayer. I, the person of little faith, began to think, what have I done!

About a week later, I saw John and asked him if he was feeling any better. He explained that the results were amazing. After he had returned home the night we prayed with him, he went to bed and woke up about midnight, and his sinuses had drained. His head was completely clear and he was in no pain at all.

Upon hearing this I felt like doing cartwheels in praise to the Lord. On the outside, I just calmly remarked how great it was that God answered our prayer. That began a long list of miracles and blessings for the House of Prayer ministry at our church; a ministry that is still going strong. In fact, I've continued to stretch beyond my comfort zone and have published a couple of articles about our prayer ministry, and I've spoken at conferences and churches about what God has done. I continue to be stretched, and am continually amazed by what God is doing in the prayer ministry. It began on a silent walk with God and I'll always be grateful for the guidance I received in those moments of quiet.

Kathy's experience makes it clear that quiet time offers us more than peace. It gives us a connection to God. Once we establish a relationship where we pray and then carefully listen for God's answer, the grace of everyday miracles will attend us.

Caring For Your Soul

: Chapter Three

THE SOUL IS A LIVING THING that is powerful and also fragile. Our soul is indestructible but it can also be weakened with a lack of care. If you lose your soul connection, it does not matter how much money you have, where you live, your level of education, or whether you are married or single. If you are not connected to your soul, you will never feel peace and will never have a sense of contentment. When someone has lost her soul connection it will show in her eyes in a vacant look, even if everything in her life seems perfect. When you see someone who is present in her eyes, you know she is in touch with her soul.

When we lose the connection to our soul we often try to fill the void from the outside. We buy a new house, we get married, we get divorced, we make changes we hope will make us feel better, or we numb the pain of disconnection with drugs and alcohol. Moving to a new state or new a country will not make a difference if the same soulless version of you continues to direct your life.

I've learned to work on matters of the spirit *first*, having faith that everything else will fall into place once a foundation with God is set.

Your Purpose

How can you act in your own best interest until you know God and know your life's purpose? This is the place to begin. With the understanding of your purpose firmly in place, you will then be ready to take action – the kind of action that will be fulfilling and that will support you in staying on track.

I believe every human being has a purpose on this planet and that this soul-purpose is written in our very DNA. A plan for our potential was put forth even before we were born. The question for each of us is, will I carry out God's plan for my life or will I work against my own agenda? Our soul's purpose should not be confused with our job or position in life. Our purpose can be fulfilled in many creative ways and in almost anything we do.

Begin with the question, why were you born? Spend time asking the question and praying and listening for an answer. Ask God, *What do you want me to do? How can I be your hands, your feet , your eyes, your ears? Who do you want me to touch during my lifetime?* Once you determine your purpose, you will know how to take care of your soul. Your purpose will act as your guide to right action.

I have a friend who was so soul sick that she said she just wanted to get in her car and drive to Canada, leaving her old life behind. If I thought she was in touch with her soul's purpose at this point, I would have encouraged her to do just that. But her cry was one of distress and she wasn't inspired about what to do next, so I offered to help her sort things out. Because this friend was a lawyer with a private practice and might be stressed out about running her own business, I checked in with another friend who was an attorney to see if she could advise our heartsick friend. The second friend, a government lawyer, was free of the stresses of making payroll and generating business, but she said that even with retirement, full insurance, and paid vacations, she didn't feel solid and safe and wasn't content.

I knew both friends worked hard and both were in very different work situations, but each told me they could not even remember the last time they had felt joy. I asked each woman what she did feel, and both described being very much out of touch with their feelings and certainly were not in touch with their souls.

As the discussions unfolded, I realized that as quickly as I made my suggestions about changes that might support a more joy-filled life, the more I heard excuses about how things couldn't be better, wouldn't change, and that this misery was just part of the career. But was that really true? I talked to a third friend, Florence, who is an immigration attorney. She explained how much she loves her work, how fulfilled she is by it, and every time she speaks about her cases I see a light in her eyes. She is full of enthusiasm, passion, and God is at work in her. It is easy to see that her professional skills and training and her soul's purpose are well-aligned and that this is what brings her joy.

It is always a soul thing. The other two lawyers who are miserable have somehow lost their soul connection and they aren't even actively trying to get it back, but are suffering unhappy lives and blaming their work as the root cause. How aligned are you with your purpose and how does your work support it? As I speak around the world, I see so many brilliant people, men and women alike, who are burned-out and who have lost their soul connection. If you have lost your soul connection, you'll need to address that issue before you begin to work on anything more "practical." Once you connect with your soul's purpose, you'll be able to see what changes to make and how to proceed, but until them go gently.

Basic Soul Care

I encourage you to make sure that every day you do something, even if it's just something small, to nourish your soul so that you are always moving in the direction of God. The frightening thing about losing a soul connection is that it can happen so incrementally that you might not even realize you are losing touch. It is like the example of putting a frog in tepid water and raising the temperature of the water so slowly that the frog does not understand it is dying. If we ignore the more subtle symptoms of being out of touch with our soul, we can find ourselves in a desperate situation.

On the other hand, daily attention to the soul brings both inward and outward joy. Here are some important ways we can nourish our soul.
» Do not be careless with your words or thoughts and don't gossip or use your words to harm others.
» Do not judge, but instead try to find compassionate connection with people, and show kindness to everyone with whom you have contact.
» Become a giver of that which you can give without being depleted, and do so with joy and generosity.
» Be patient and slow to anger, process and release anger, and be tolerant and understanding of yourself and others, and learn to wait on the Lord.
» Make sure your words and deeds are congruent and honest.
» Show pure love to yourself and to everyone else and offer forgiveness easily.
» Honor your connection to God and give it importance in your life.

I try to remember that what I put in my mind is just as important as what I put in my body. I know that junk food and junk thoughts are not soul nourishing, but that good books always lift my spirit. My purse is a mobile library. I always have a book with me. I read every where I go, while waiting in line, or waiting for a meeting to start. Sometimes, when someone else is late for a meeting I don't even realize it, because I am lost in an inspiring book. I listen to good music and books on tape in my car, and the time I could spend just "getting around" is time that instead takes me higher.

When Others Aren't On the Same Page

I am often asked how we can be loving toward others who don't share the same desire to live a Godly life we do. How can we respect them, yet not allow them to bring us down? We know that our most important connection is with God. Once that relationship is in order, we are ready to look with gentleness at ourselves and at those around us. I've learned that speaking about what I'm trying to do in my life to people who don't share these interests is not fruitful and leaves me feeling too exposed. On the other hand, I don't want to live in ways that are not authentic, or miss opportunities to speak about sacred matters in ways that will inspire others.

Your inner guidance will help you know what to say and when to say it, and the more you tune into your soul, the more you'll be guided in all things. If you need to extend your circle to include more people who share your interests, you'll find this a great way to build support for living a soulful life. Sometimes, not only do we need to change our inner dialogue with ourselves and God, but we also need to shift our environment and change even the people we hang out with. There are some incredibly negative people out there who can drain energy and cause us to lose power and life force very quickly. I've found that I can lovingly and prayerfully release them, without having to confront them, and that they just move gently out of my life.

Trusting God

It is possible that even though you are working hard, you feel you have nothing to show for your effort. When you have done all you can, just wait and trust. God is already working in your favor and he does not work with linear time. There is no yesterday or tomorrow – all is the same to God. Scripture tells us to turn things over to God and when we do we experience grace and everyday miracles.

The things that test and try us can be a powerful catalyst for change and so we can honor the struggle. I learned important lessons about taking care of my soul when my father died. My grief was hard to bear, but at my father's funeral not only did I hear about his religious faith, but I also heard from people he had helped directly, and the lessons of his life changed mine. My father did not have a lot of money, but he was still generous. He did not put off giving until he was in a position to do so easily – he gave based on what he had at that moment and he trusted in God.

A Sacred Promise

During my growing up, I saw my parents practice unconditional giving. They gave money, they gave advice and time. To this day, my mother is a wonderful listener and her prayers for people and her concern for them is an important part of her soul's purpose and her ministry. From her, I have learned to do something for my soul every day and to operate from the level of the soul in everything I do.

When we make a sacred promise to attend to our soul, we ask daily questions. Am I walking in integrity? Am I demonstrating with this act that I am my sister and my brother's keeper? Did I show love to someone today? Am I acting in ways that are consistent with my soul's purpose? It is a constant soulful inquiry. On any day, when the answer to these questions lets us know that we have not done our best, we can continue to affirm the sacred promise and be gentle with ourselves. We can try to do better tomorrow and stay in close contact with God. Practicing forgiveness calls us to forgive ourselves and to simply commit to trying again. There are always great lessons to be learned in the cycle of striving, failing, succeeding, recommitting, and making progress.

Vera Thomas is someone who made a sacred promise and now works to keep it. She does this with great humanity and courage. Her story is a perfect illustration of the challenges and joys of caring for the soul. She writes:

in Amber's life, and how much more I could help her attend to her soul. Amber is my niece by marriage. She had previously lived with me for about six years prior to the time I divorced her uncle. In July, on a dreary summer day, when rain brought sheets of humidity, there she stood at my door. I knew about her present situation but had not seen her in person to confirm it. Amber was showing her pregnancy at six months and was only fifteen years old. Her eyes were weary and pain was evident even in her voice. She spoke softly and sadly, "Can I come in?"

At first, I wanted no part of this ordeal. Her uncle and I had been separated for over a year. Amber and I had only been related through marriage and I had just begun to pick up the pieces from my own broken life. I had sacrificed a four-bedroom home, a level of financial security, the luxury of family vacations, and the ability to continue to be a stay-at-home mom. But it had been worth it for the peace-of-mind I felt. My children and I were starting over with just the minimum – a small home in a remote area, government assistance, and a budget tighter than the lid of grandma's canned peaches. But I felt nothing but gratitude knowing that I had a chance to live again, this time for God and not for man. Every day brought new strength and drew me that much closer to the unchanging love of God.

But here was Amber, and she was hungry, helpless, and homeless. It hurt my spirit to see her in such a desperate situation. With everything I had, I wanted to help her, but the past can affect even the tenderest situations and allow doubt and fear to settle in and fester.

Amber and I had a rocky past. She had often criticized me and my methods for trying to raise her when she had lived with us. She had complained about me to anybody who had ears. Was I a terrible caregiver? No. I just wanted for Amber what nobody had ever given me. I thought she needed to be raised according to God's word. There were rules and guidelines in my household that she had to follow. I expected her to get good grades, I wouldn't allow phone calls from boys without my permission, household chores had to be done and church was a privilege not a punishment. Well, in this day and age all of that seemed "old school." She felt my guidelines were harsh and that I was keeping her away from the world.

The truth was that I hadn't far left the places that she would have to journey through. And since she had lost her mother to drug and alcohol abuse, you'd think the world would be the last place she'd look to for guidance. I was convinced that if I had received half the raising she had been getting with me, life would have dealt me a much better hand. I was trying to save her from the life I had led. Amber tried every trick of the trade to bypass my rules, but as every parent would say, "You can't pull that over me. I've tried everything you've tried and then some." When her uncle and I separated, he left her behind. This had been an abusive relationship and his intentions were clearly to leave me helpless with our three children and Amber, so that I wouldn't be able to make it on my own and would have to take him back. That didn't happen. My ex had been physically, mentally, and emotionally abusive for ten years. And one day, I drew enough strength to say, "Enough is enough!" The determination I found in my new connection to God became my strength. Nothing could make me stay. I decided I'd rather live in a box and have a peace of mind than to stay in that mess! So I left. I packed what I could in a duffle bag, grabbed on to the love of my children and ran as fast as I could. Amber had remained with me six months after the ordeal of leaving.

Emotionally, I was a wreck at the beginning. I became withdrawn and felt flat. I often-times closed off from the world and hid in solitude. Amber, didn't understand. She thought that I was neglectful and that I didn't want her around. Amber decided my actions toward her were personal rather than pitiful. So, she found a way to locate her estranged dad of fourteen years and began to complain to him about having to live with me.

One cool Monday in October, when the leaves were just beginning to fall from the trees, Amber withdrew from school at his request. She had secretly packed her belongings over the weekend and left to live with her father. He had made promises to her about their new life together and she was excited. Very soon, she found that all of his promises were lies. There was no new life for her, but instead a hatred that had built up between them. He left her abandoned with a family she did not know and in living conditions she was not accustomed to. She was supposed to cook and clean for three other children near her same age and share a bed and her clothes with them.

Many times, the children were left in the house by themselves, and Amber also had to deal with frightening verbal abuse. As for her dad, he would disappear for weeks at a time until eventually he wasn't around at all. Of course, she wanted to come back and live with me but there wasn't much that I could do. Once her dad got legal custody, I had no rights. Besides, we were barely making it ourselves. I was making ends meet out of ends meat. I was spending more that I was bringing in and battling in court with my ex over everything from the mattress to the mortgage. I was uncontrollably losing weight, losing my hair from the stress, and undoubtedly my mind. Stability wasn't something I could give her when I hadn't acquired it yet myself.

That is when it happened. She met "the guy" who was going to take all her troubles away. What she didn't realize was that no one can shelter you from the storm like the Lord, but she wasn't using that umbrella, so the storm was going to rip through her life. Honestly, I was in that same storm at the same time, had the umbrella in hand, but failed to use it.

So, there we stood on each side of my doorway. Amber wet from the summer rain, and I from the puddle of tears that soaked my cotton blouse. As I looked in her sorrowful brown eyes, I saw a very young version of myself. I had experienced so many doors slamming in my face with no one to let me in and guide me. I had to learn on my own the hard way. I knew I needed to do something for Amber. I couldn't let her life continue to be a mirror of my own. We had lost so much. It was time to reclaim what was rightfully ours.

I stepped away from the entrance and let her in. We embraced one another like never before. Her heart pounded against mine and the life growing inside her danced from her cries. "God," I prayed aloud, "guide us and strengthen us. Bless this journey that we are about to embark on together and keep us tuned in to your voice and vision. We need you to stand in the gap. Heal our wounds and restore our hearts. And most of all, Lord, thank you for bringing Amber back to me and her soul back to her. The road may be dangerous and the waters may be rough, but, dearest Lord, steer the course of our lives and guide us to salvation. Amen."

The last time I heard from them, Vera and Amber were doing just fine – and so is the lovely baby girl who blesses their home. Amber is on the honor roll at school and calls Vera "Mom," in honor of the role she so powerfully took on that rainy night. They are both living the truth that care of the soul is the first priority, the best way to solve problems, and the only way to get grounded in this world. We all build up from that.

Guard your soul like the treasure it is and use it as a rudder to steer your life. The grace we find in each day comes through love of ourselves and others, and most importantly, to our connection with our Creator.

Angel on My Shoulder

IT SEEMS FITTING THAT ANGELS have such a welcome place in world-wide culture these days. We see representations of angels all around us, and if we pay daily attention to this symbol of divine connection, we may discover that we are really are protected and guided by a loving presence. We may also find that these angels can be seen in the form of people who act kindly toward us.

We have all heard about God moments when real angels have appeared to save someone from harm, or ministered to someone in need. I have never had that kind of literal angel experience myself, but I have felt many moments when I was guided and protected, and when I felt carried along by the presence of some loving force that I can only describe as angelic. There are times when this presence is so real that I feel I could close my eyes and open my arms wide and hug my guardian angel.

Carried On The Wings of Angels

When we experience moments of fear and doubt, we have an opportunity to turn those moments into angel moments instead. I'm nervous when I fly, and so I have never taken a plane ride without asking God to send angels to be with me. I've been comforted in this way since I was a child; my mother prayed for us as the last thing she did before any of us traveled. When I pray, I always feel that I have been given the gift of calm in return. These small angel moments can be a part of our lives every day, if only we invite them.

It is also possible for us to move beyond feeling the presence of angels around us, and to become an angel for someone else in this world. I often ask myself, "Whose angel can I be? When was the last time I helped someone without expecting anything in return? When have I helped someone when it was not the easiest thing to do, but the hardest?"

As I grew up, I saw my parents act as angels for others all the time. They gave comfort and aid even to strangers, and I learned from them that sometimes it is the small and simple acts of service that matter most. It could be stopping to give someone who is obviously lost the directions that will help her on her way, even when you are in a terrible rush yourself. And often, acts of kindness that are done privately are the most wonderful. I am always deeply touched when gifts come from an anonymous source, from someone who does not want anything in return and who is not seeking recognition for what he has done. That feels like love in action to me.

I hope the story that follows will inspire you to pay the toll of the person driving up to the toll booth behind you. I hope it will invite you to see the needs of others around you and to respond generously. Today is a day you can be someone's angel, reminding her that the world is a loving place and that God's love surrounds us all. Sharon Beth Brani and her little daughter learned that they were not alone when an angel was near at hand.

When I adopted my daughter as a single mom, I knew that it would be difficult financially. I had no idea how difficult. Although my teaching job provided steady income, it was modest, and the post-adoption costs of taking care of my daughter continued to rise. One month in particular, things were terribly tight. I paid the bills and looked at what was left for us. Absolutely nothing.

I looked at my precious little toddler and felt the pain of not being able to provide for her properly as we faced the coldest winter in many years. It's was January and her tender little legs needed warm tights. Taking my child anywhere was challenging in the cold, and a few people at church had even pointed out to me that her legs needed more to cover them.

"Lord, what can I do? You have promised to provide for the orphans and the widows," I cried out loud and the pain in my soul was great. I heard no voice in response. No answer came. For the rest of the day, my heart was heavy with sadness and that night I felt abandoned.

The next morning, I opened the front door and the cold wind hit my face. At my feet was a large brown paper bag stuffed with answers to my cry. "What in the world," I said, taking out a little girl's dress that was the perfect size for my daughter. My heart leapt with excitement. "Who in the world," I whispered aloud. The bag was full of warm pants, shirts, sweaters, and shoes. Item after item was just the right size, and at the bottom of the bag were pairs of tights – warm, colorful tights in every shade of the rainbow.

My happy tears fell as I searched for some identification of the giver. There was none. Just a generous bag filled with everything a mother could want for her child. "Thank you, Lord, for sending your special angel with this bag," I whispered. When my daughter awoke and toddled into the room, she found her mother sitting on the floor surrounded by piles of pretty clothes. "Who give?" she struggled to say.
"Your angel," I answered. "Your angel left them at the door." Her face lit up with delight. From then on, a bag would appear at our door every so often. The bags were filled with clothes, toys, shoes, and many useful and beautiful things for my daughter, and always in her size. We were both comforted by these gifts. As long as there is a God, we know there are angels to watch over us. Knowing this has brought us great peace.

Whoever the angel was who attended so wonderfully to Sharon and her daughter, they must have known that they were bringing joy, comfort, and love. That seems like the perfect way to define an angel moment – a time when we feel full of joyfulness and are comforted by being surrounded with love. For many of us, this definition of angel can be extended to a special animal that provided gifts of love and comfort. This next story comes from Debbie Willows, who is a gifted writer and speaker and a world-record holder and two-time Paralympian. Debbie was born with Cerebral Palsy and was told she would never walk, speak, or graduate from high school. But Debbie and God had other plans and she pushed herself through school, typing with a pen held in her teeth, and finally graduated with honors. Debbie challenged herself to swim and worked hard to excel as an athlete. She has traveled the world, winning many medals for Canada, and loves spending time with her ten nieces and nephews. Debbie feels she was given the gift of a very special angel in the form of her service dog, Lego.

I sat on my porch overlooking the park on a cool evening in June and watched people walking their dogs, while I grieved the loss of mine. As the shadows grew longer, I tried to come to terms with the events of the past few hours. My helper, companion, and friend had just died. We had spent the past ten years together and were inseparable. My heart felt like shattered glass as I remembered him.

I received this big, black, standard poodle on a sunny afternoon in June of 1993. Lego was two years old and came bounding into my home and into my heart, changing my life forever. I had waited for years and now I had my four-legged bundle of energy and support. Cerebral Palsy made me unable to walk or use my hands productively. I had applied to the Lions Foundation in Oakville, Ontario, for one of the dogs they trained for people with disabilities. It had taken two years for them to train Lego and now it was time for us to start with the basics as a team.

We had to learn to trust each other. The two trainers who helped with the transition showed me how to walk him, feed him, play with him, and then how to work with him. The trainers spent several days with us, showing me how to do something with Lego and then leaving us for a few hours while we practiced. Each day was more exciting; as I saw Lego's abilities grow and my limitations fall away as I received his assistance.

After the trainers had done their job, they left. I was assured of their future visits and knew their help was only a phone call away, but still I was a bit overwhelmed with fear. My fear didn't last long, as Lego and I plunged into our new life together. With his help, I could finally live on my own, and Lego seemed to know this was our place, as he laid claim to the couch. He was always ready for action when he heard the click of my power chair motors.

Lego was by my side 24/7 and we did everything together. With Lego as my companion, I was able to do many more things that I could do on my own. He saved me time and frustration and gave me freedom. I could go to the mall with Lego walking proudly in harness beside me. If I dropped something, he would pick it up and gently place it on my lap. He would push the buttons that opened doors, give the store clerk my wallet and bring it back to me. He even flew on airplanes with me, sometimes getting better service than I received. We went to church, and even the movies. One time, sitting quietly watching a movie together, he reached over the seat in front of us and sniffed the man's arm. The man jumped so high in his surprise, I thought he was going to hit the ceiling!

At bedtime, I trained Lego to turn off the light and close the door. I gave him a treat after doing this. One night, Lego turned on the light at two a.m. and stood by the light switch proudly wagging his tail and waiting for his treat! He lived to eat, and had a great sense of humor and the blessings he gave my life were too numerous to count. Lego's chocolate brown eyes melted my heart each time he helped me. He seemed to know he was my angel.

Lego was not perfect. We had our challenges. He was, after all, a dog – a fact I had to remind him of on many occasions. One of his faults, or gifts, depending on how you looked at it, was his ability to steal food. Lego was tall enough to walk by a table and very quickly take a bun without you seeing him. He was very stealthy in this regard and it got him into trouble when he grabbed and ate something that disagreed with him. One day, after Lego had grabbed and eaten something that made him sick, I cried out in frustration, "Lego, if you love me, why do you do this!" The question haunted me later, because I realized that all of us do things that aren't good for us sometimes. I wondered if God was asking me the same question, challenging me to be less stubborn and to do what he asked of me, knowing it was for my benefit.

As old age finally crept up on him, Lego seemed to cling to me. He needed my help now. His hearing failed and he lost interest in eating. He still knew when I was sick or feeling down and would stay close by or climb onto my bed.

On our last day together, Lego's back legs gave out and he dragged himself on his belly to be close to me. I looked in his eyes and knew our time together as a team had come to an end. I took him to the clinic, where he collapsed again. The staff tried to make him comfortable, being very kind and gentle as they confirmed what I already knew: it was time for him to go. Lego looked so peaceful when he left that it seemed he would get up any minute. But I knew he was really gone when my power chair motors clicked and he made no response.

I grieved in the moonlight flooding my porch that night, as an orchestra of crickets played. Friends joined me for a time of reminiscing and support, and together we talked, laughed, and cried as we remembered Lego's life.

My heart still aches, but I will always cherish our years together and the joy God brought to me through this angel of a dog. I now have a companion dog named Tate, a younger version of Lego, who is working hard to learn all that his predecessor had done for me. He's a good dog who will learn and love in his own way. But there will only ever be one Lego, the angel who taught me to love, laugh, and enjoy life in a unique and special way.

Angels In A Time of Need

When we need God he is there in the form of a stranger, a family member, an answered prayer, and anywhere else we see His hand. When Char McCargo Bah became deathly ill in a far away land, she was comforted by the words of another faith, as well as by her own faith and by her connection to her grandmother.

In 1988, my husband Mumini and my very young daughter Maimoona and I lived in Sierra Leone, West Africa for a time. Before we left the United States and again upon our arrival in West Africa, we took precautions so that we would not contract malaria. Could the doctors protect us against those especially big and dangerous mosquitoes in West Africa? I hoped so.

The three of us visited my mother-in-law in a town called Sefadu in the Kono district. Returning from the market one day, I felt tired and weak, but since I had the fewest mosquito bites among us, neither I nor my husband suspected that I had contracted malaria. The next day, my husband had to travel to the capital of Sierra Leone, Freetown, about two-hundred miles from the town in which we were staying. He needed to be gone for two weeks. It would be a challenging time for me and my young daughter because my mother-in-law and two nieces did not speak English. We would have to communicate as best we could in Krio-pidgin English and with hand gestures.

A day after my husband left for Freetown, I felt every symptom of malaria: high temperature, sweating, and chills. My clothes were saturated with sweat. I could not hold any food down and every smell nauseated me. I also had diarrhea and was becoming severely dehydrated. I had my niece dip cloth into a bucket of cold water and I rubbed it over my body to try and get the fever down. There was no thermometer to check my temperature, but my mother-in-law touched my forehead and called God's name.

I needed to see a doctor, but access to any clinic was impossible because no one in the family had a car. I understood that I would have to fight this illness without medical help. I started hallucinating. The pretty yellow flowers printed on the bed sheet appeared to be attacking me. I tried to squash the flowers with my palms, but still they came at me. I became so sick I could not fight the flowers anymore and I felt myself drifting into a tunnel that had light at the very end. I heard voices from my past and revisited memories of growing up.

In the background, I heard Islamic prayers being said by someone. I started praying myself, asking God not to take me. I remember telling Him the reasons I wanted to stay on earth longer. I wanted to see my daughter grow up, go to college and marry. I also knew my husband would not forgive himself if I died in Sierra Leone. I promised God that I would be obedient to Him if I lived. After all the praying the light I saw at the end of the tunnel grew dim. But I could still see and hear an old lady praying and could tell it was my maternal grandmother standing in the tunnel saying her prayers and motioning me to go back to life. My grandmother had been dead since 1978, but she appeared very real to me as she encouraged me to live.

After days had gone by, I opened my eyes and saw that my mother-in-law was sitting on the edge of my bed reading Quranic verses and praying for me. I realized that God had given me two Angels from two different religions to pray on each side of the tunnel. I knew they both helped me get me through the ordeal.

My nieces squeezed some orange juice that I finally managed to keep down, and after several more days, I started getting my strength back. When my husband returned and saw how ill I still looked and that I had lost over twenty pounds, he knew I had experienced a close encounter with death. It soon became clear to us that another of the gifts of those two weeks was that I built a strong bond with my mother-in-law and nieces and that together we had connected as a family.

Reflecting on my experiences in Sierra Leone and other life experiences that followed, I know that prayer and a connection to ancestors can make a difference. In 1995, my mother-in-law joined my maternal grandmother. It was a difficult time for all of us, especially my husband. But I feel both of these women watching over us now.

Learning to Receive an Angel Moment

It is a lesson I find myself having to learn over and over again – that we have to be open in order to receive gifts from God. When we shut down, are deeply discouraged and without faith, and when we complain bitterly, we are not able to receive an angel moment. Karen Ward is an independent woman who once preferred to give rather than receive, but on an average sort of day, in the midst of regular life events, she found ways to be more open to receiving the things she needed most and learned that giving and receiving have a wonderful kind of balance.

This morning I was awakened at five by my two-year-old. I attended to him and then crawled back into bed trying to sneak in a few more minutes of sleep. When my husband left for work, I started making lunches in the kitchen. The clock on the microwave told me I was still ahead of schedule for the day, and I was pleased.

A few moments later, I happened to look at a different clock. It was forty-five minutes later than the microwave clock, and I knew this was the accurate time. I was mortified to realize that I was going to be late. I rushed to help out in the classroom, as I do on Mondays, knowing that although I really had to go to the supermarket, I had made an appointment to see an old friend later that morning. I rang her hoping she'd want to cancel, but she said she needed to see me.

I confess I was annoyed to be behind schedule. I had a long "to do" list for the day, and this stop to be with a friend, however pleasant, was getting in the way! I was a little ashamed of my attitude, but not enough to get my act together.

I determined to spend no longer than half an hour with my friend. That way, I could get the shopping done afterwards and get my youngest home in time for his nap. An hour later, our boys had just started to play nicely together while I spent time with her, and despite feeling guilty about my "to do" list, I was enjoying catching up with this Godly woman. It was doing us all some good, but still I insisted that it was time to go. I mentioned that we were going to the shops and since the boys were obviously not happy to be pulled away from their games, my friend offered to mind them while I shopped.

Immediately I said "Oh, no. Thanks, but we'll be fine." Then, just as she was saying "Are you sure?" I asked myself why I was being so stubborn. Why would I refuse this generous and genuine offer? It was a big step for me to accept. I took pride in being independent and not needing anything from anyone, now I realized it was pride that didn't serve me well. My friend said she would give them all lunch so my youngest would be ready for his nap as soon as I returned. She was so thoughtful and I was so grateful!

I walked out to my car and hopped in. I was about to turn the key in the ignition when I stopped, bowed my head and said, "Father, you are so generous to me when I let you be! Thank you!"
My shopping was done in half the time it usually takes, and my children had a delightful time. My friend made an open offer to mind them

whenever I need to shop. I will accept again soon and I will appreciate the gift and will pass it on.

Open Your Heart

If we feel more comfortable giving than receiving we miss the opportunity to feel the blessings of receiving. This gives us another reason to slow down and listen. Lately I have been praying that God will help me to listen to him more. I used to pray so intensely, begging God to speak and often feeling like he didn't. Then I realized I was doing all the talking. A good friend told me, "God never stops talking, you just need to listen." My recent experience has taught me that this is very true and that listening is all that is required to hear Him. How could our creator, who spoke the world into being, keep silent? Instead of earnestly and fervently begging and beseeching, I'm trying to learn how to open my heart and my ears. It seems to be working.

We have to be willing to receive our angel moments as well as to give angel moments. This simple story from Pam Hirson illustrates the joy of receiving and reminds us to invite help into our lives.

I vowed that nothing would erode my serenity today, not even a raging winter storm. The snow was falling heavily and fast, the kids were with their father for the weekend, and my mother was resting, and so I could claim this day for myself. This would be a day of tranquility.

There was more snow-shoveling work than I could handle physically, but I decided not to let the snow interfere with my sense of peace. I would try not to worry or give in to fear. Not even fear about my mother's illness. She was sleeping in her room, and I hoped that the power wouldn't go out, or that we would run out of her oxygen. I briefly imagined rescue vehicles trying to plow through mounds of snow, but realized there wasn't anything I could do. *Please Lord, fill me with your peace.*

It wasn't easy for me to release my worries and responsibilities. I felt the financial strain of being a single parent and the pressures of taking care of my mother. I often felt like I was sinking. In the past few months, when I found myself short on ideas, and long on need, I turned to my friend, Janine, who shared stories about her life and her faith with me. She seemed so together, yet in her difficult circumstances I didn't see how she could be. "What's your secret?" I asked her. "Secret?" She sounded perplexed. "I look at you and see a woman who has a lot on her plate and yet you seem undaunted. How do you do that?" "I give it to God." "I don't understand." "Faith is the opposite of worry. Naturally, I feel overwhelmed at times. That's when I need to pray more. And when I do, it's like releasing my cares. I know they're in good hands and that God is already working on the best possible outcome for me. It's about trusting Him to do for me what I can't do for myself." "It sounds so simple, but somehow I doubt it is." "Pray, pray, and then pray some more; eventually you begin to feel the peace that only God can bring you. The more you pray, the greater the peace. Develop a relationship with God as the most significant relationship in your life. Put Him first, and everything else will fall into place."

Lacking any viable alternatives, I started to give faith a try. I relied on her guidance as she introduced me to her prayer group. At first I was shy and just sat quietly and listened. There were so many stories, so many miracles. They called it a testimony and hope and faith filled the room as they shared their experiences. Janine and I discussed miracles, prayers, and bible passages. Slowly, I started to find my way. I learned how to see God working in my life. And then I felt myself believing. That's when I accepted Him and realized He had been there all along.

On that snowy day I was trying to put my growing faith in practice in a new way. By three o'clock snow had already blanketed the street. It wasn't slowing down. No one was out. I worried again. *What am I going to do?* And my new-found faith whispered, *Don't worry. I trust you to dig me out of this, somehow, Father.*

I settled at the dining room table and sipped herbal tea. Through the window, I watch the heavy flakes as they continued to fall. A gentle knock on the front door startled me. Wrapped in flannel and fleece, I opened the door to find a neighbor who had trekked here from his home down the block. He was bundled from head to toe. I didn't know him, except for the passing waves of greeting we sometimes exchanged. Hi," he said. "Your mailbox blew open and your mail was lying in the snow. "Thank you so much." I smiled appreciatively.

"No problem," he said. And I was warmed and cheered by his simple act of kindness.

My mother was sound asleep in front of the television and looked comfortable for now. I opened a book, but my eyes wandered to the window and the snow. The whir of a motor came to life. What in the world was that? Born and raised a city girl, it was not a familiar sound. I peeked from behind the blinds to find the same neighbor with a snow blower clearing my sidewalk and driveway. Delight filled my heart. It was as if God Himself was offering assistance. *Thank you, Father.* I rushed to the phone to tell Janine.

Excitedly I blurted, "All this snow and I was so worried. I didn't know how I would ever shovel out. I tried to stay calm, I talked to God, and wham, just like that, He did it. He took care of me in the midst of this storm." "Whoa. Slow down. What do you mean?"

"He sent me an angel with a snow blower."

"Oh Pam, that's amazing; I love how He works."

As I hung up the phone, giddiness stayed with me. I felt wonderful. I finally understood how prayer works. I didn't need a special place or time to speak to God. No appointment was necessary. He was always there, even when I was snowbound.

I engage in a dialogue with God often now. My side of the conversation is verbal, but His comes in many forms. Sometimes, He just plants a seed in the heart of someone else and it's a gift to me. Just like the day He sent a Snow Angel.

Be An Angel to a Stranger

There is a homeless man on Miami Beach who is a friend of mine. He knows my name and I know his because we have a connection. I started giving him a dollar even when I was looking for a dollar myself. It just felt right to me to do it. I felt guided to help him in the small ways I could.

At first, I would hand him a dollar without speaking to him, but that didn't seem right. When I looked in his eyes, asked his name, and told him it was nice to meet him, things felt right between us. He asked my name, and from then out we could greet each other properly. This man is a precious child of God and I know that. I also know we can follow our sense of when to be wisely wary of people, and also be open to knowing when to connect and help people – in all of the ways we feel inspired to be their angels. When we give, not out of a sense of obligation or guilt, but with a real desire to make a difference, we act for God.

Dinorah Blackman wrote to me from Panama, sharing her story of being helped by a stranger. It is a reminder to me that grace attends even the most mundane aspects of our lives – even just getting around.

I had just enjoyed a blessed time at church. It was one of those occasions when evening comes and you look back and say, "It has been a truly wonderful day!" The music was beautiful, the conversation was good, and my cup had been filled to overflowing.

I was a little tired and still needed to drive about twenty miles home. The road itself was in good condition, but much of it was unlit, winding and steep. Motorists were forced to slow down and accidents often occurred on this stretch of road.

I stopped at a service station to fill my tank. It was already getting dark. I wanted to be on my way as quickly as possible. As I drove up to the pump, I noticed a very old man sitting on a stool. Although he was wearing the overalls of a mechanic, he seemed too old to be working. He walked to my car, looked me straight in the eye, and tapped the hood, indicating that I should open it. Without hesitating, I obeyed and then watched as he disappeared under the hood and then emerged with the coolant bottle in his hands. With flourish he removed the cover, and turned it over so I could see how dry it was.

How could he have known? The motor wasn't smoking; it wasn't making any strange sounds. He filled the bottle, gave me a little smile and walked back to his seat. I took care of my bill and just before driving off, I looked where this beautiful old man had been seated. He was no longer there. I wasn't surprised.

I was relieved that I wouldn't be stranded alone on a dark and mountainous road. There were tears of gratitude in my eyes as I drove away. In my hurry, I had forgotten to tell the man thank you. In total humility, I sang my gratitude to my God, and I know He relayed the message.

Expect the Unexpected

If we do not expect the unexpected, we will miss our angel moment. I first heard God whisper those words to me while on a bus on the way to Atlanta to speak. It was the middle of the night and I was in the middle of nowhere going from Miami to Atlanta. I had just started speaking to groups and had a sense I was doing the right thing, but I needed to pay my way in life and so I hoped my calling would provide a living, if I kept moving forward in faith. The organizers of the event could not afford to pay me, so I told them I would speak free of charge and that I would even pay my own way to Atlanta. I had no money, but I kept hoping and praying for the unexpected. I did not know where it was going to come from, but it did have to happen.

The telephone company owed me some money, but when I called, I found I wouldn't be getting a check for a month. I was due in Atlanta in five days. A voice inside told me to check my mailbox. At this time in my life, my mailbox was often full of bills I couldn't pay and that frightened me. I didn't have money, so I avoided the mailbox. All day, the Holy Spirit kept telling me to check my mail box and when I finally did there was a check for two-hundred dollars inside. I could take the bus to Atlanta, but would have no money for anything else. I continued to pray, and the same voice told me to go and check my mailbox again the next day. This time, there was a check for two-thousand dollars.

I kept feeling the encouragement to move in a new direction and felt God telling me that if I created something truly useful for people, they would come. What happened at the seminar in Atlanta? Over six hundred people showed up, and together we celebrated the decision to change. I heard from many people after that event. The work had helped men and women make an important shift in their lives, and I had also learned something important – to expect the unexpected.

Counting On God

We turn to God in times of trouble, we turn to Him in times of triumph, and we certainly count on Him when we are engaged in His work. Lucy Cain found everyday miracles when she gave the gift of her service.

"Mama, I have to go to Belize!" These were the words that sparked a wonderful chain of events in our lives. After hearing a presentation about a mission trip to Belize, Central America, our daughter Emily asked us if she could go. I was nervous because she was only sixteen, but when God calls you into mission work, you know it! She felt called to serve and so she went. For two years in a row, Emily went to Belize with a ministry as a summer camp counselor working with visually impaired children and adults. Camp was held in a monastery near the border with Guatemala.

After seeing her pictures and hearing her testimonies about how God had worked on these trips, my husband Johnny and I felt the call to go with her on the next trip. Our team was prepared to provide eye clinics in schools and villages around Punta Gorda, Belize. Johnny would be part of the construction crew that would build a new youth outreach center. We soon experienced the testimony that special "things happen" on mission trips. Things we could not explain, other than we were seeing God at work.

When we arrived in Belize City on that hot November day we were presented with two passenger vans to use as our transportation for the week. We'd met our first challenge. The vans looked and acted as if they could barely function, and we needed to rely on them to cover many miles through remote areas.

Our missionary eye doctor drove a group of us into one of the Mayan villages to conduct his clinic. We had an incredibly blessed day attending to the needs of beautiful and happy people. Emily and I, along with a group of special ladies, worked with adorable children in their classrooms, and during recess and lunch breaks we joined in Bible stories, playing with puppets and singing songs.

When the clinic was finished for the day, we piled in the van to head down the mountain to Punta Gorda. At the top of the mountain, our driver suddenly stopped and explained that we needed to pray for the van. The brakes were totally gone and we were stranded at the top of the steep mountain trail with no phones. It was just us and God at the end of the day. We prayed and prayed, and doctor who was driving us sat there a minute quietly. When he decided to go, we felt confident that God was with us, and we started down the hill and felt the brakes engage once again!

A few days later, God gave us another miracle. One of our tasks was to paint the exterior and interior of a new concrete bathhouse, which was adjacent to the outreach center building another group in our team was working on. We had several gallons of paint, but found that concrete soaks up the first coat or two.

There were about six of us painting away, and, after a few hours, we realized that we were definitely not going to have enough paint and the paint store was four hours away. Time was running out, and we didn't have the luxury to take a long trip for paint. We decided we'd keep going to see how far we could get with what we had left, and pray.

He heard our prayers and we kept painting. When we finished, we realized that we had enough paint and that there was even an extra gallon that we hadn't even opened. Many wonderful things happened on this trip and on a following trip, when we returned to help with dental clinics in the villages.

When God calls you to go, be prepared. He won't let you rest until you do, and He will bless you greatly. You can expect to experience things that will knock your socks off. Things you will remember for a lifetime.

Angel Until The End

I met my friend Chaya Srivatsa in London in 2004 when I spoke at a women's conference there. The next year, we spent time together in Singapore at a conference where we were both speakers. Over the years, we have remained friends. I asked her to contribute a story of her choosing in this book, and was grateful when she decided to share a very intimate experience. Chaya takes us into the world of the kind of service that is often required by caregivers who attend to their loved ones. Her story is about what it takes to be an angel until the end.

It was an ordinary day just like any other day in my life – with a huge difference. On this day, Srivatsa, my husband, went for a medical check-up. He hated those things. Always a healthy man with a disciplined lifestyle, he was a typical retired service officer. He was up at five in the morning and on the golf course at day break. Ramrod straight, he would walk the eighteen holes, pulling his own cart, playing a gentlemen's game, a stickler for rules and very honestly recording his scores on the card he dropped in the box at the club. He had no patience for medicine and he had a phobia about injections. That is why I was surprised when he wanted our son, Arjun, to have him "checked out" as he put it. Arjun had recommended an MRI.

I went to work as usual and returned home for lunch. Srivatsa was in the bathroom taking a shower and my daughter-in-law Chetana, who had accompanied him for the MRI, insisted that I eat since I am diabetic and need food at regular intervals. I chatted with her about work and she was a patient listener. Arjun joined us with the MRI reports and carefully studied them. "Is everything fine, baby?" I asked him, expecting him to say that all was well. But he said something that shattered my life in an instant. "No, Mum. Dad has a tumor in his brain."

I had a cold and numb feeling in the pit of the stomach. I wanted to hear that it was just a small and well-contained intruder that could be cut out and thrown away and we could get on with our lives. "I have asked Dr. Sridhar to operate next Friday," he said, hugging me tightly. Not usually a demonstrative person, his gesture told me how worried he was. He was holding me protectively. I looked up to see his eyes brimming with tears. "I have called Anil and he is arriving with Deepali and the children on Monday." So the brothers had organized everything before breaking the news to me. This was very bad; it was clear our world was shaken at the foundation.

I went to my prayer room and cried, seeking God's help to cope. I did not want Srivatsa to suffer any pain, but all I could do was to shower my husband with the same love and affection that had been the heart of our marriage for over four decades.

A year after the surgery, he struggled and I sat by him, reading a book on Karma theory, watching television with him, or simply sharing memories of the lovely years we had spent together. He held my hand in a tight grip, unable now to express what he felt. His days were spent in a deep sleep and occasionally he would surface to flash a weak smile. Humming "Teddy bear, teddy bear, brush your teeth," I moved the battery operated toothbrush in his mouth, coaxing him to say "aaaaaah." Bathing times were fun, as I trained the hand shower on his body pretending he was a plant and that I was tending him like a gardener. Dabbing baby powder under his arms and getting him into his clothes, I planted a kiss on his cheek and tucked him in for his morning nap, while I went to make his breakfast porridge.

I loved spooning food into his mouth, cajoling the way I do with my grandchildren to get him to show me his "tiger mouth," wiping a morsel hovering on his lips. Every day I hoped he would say something new, every day I was challenged to interpret his gestures and sounds. I ask him to recite Jack and Jill from the part of his memory that he still had, and I clapped when he got the rhyme right.

There were no more parties for us, no more dancing to beloved melodies on Saturday nights, and no more holidays with our family. But there were also no regrets. A Sanskrit verse spells out the various roles of a wife, and George Bernard Shaw summed them up similarly as mistress, companion, and nurse. I was my husband's mistress when we were young. I was seductive and attractive to him and he to me. In our middle years I was his companion and participated in all of his activities. It was a hectic, exciting, and fulfilling time for us. And now, I am his nurse in old age as he sleeps, breathing gently, and I attend to him like a mother, adding that role like a signature at the end of the romantic love letter of our marriage.

When he finally did go, I poured the drop of Holy Ganga water into Sri's mouth. He looked as peaceful as he did when he slept. My son Anil, who had just stepped out to answer the doorbell, walked in to see me stroking his father's forehead. "He has gone," I whispered. My eyes seemed dry after the months of crying. I called my grandchildren in the room. All four of them tiptoed in. "Is grandpa never coming back?" asked five year-old Soorya. His seven year-old sister Kavya hugged him and whispered, "No, he has gone to God." Eleven year-old Nikita understood and hugged me, tears choking her. Karan, all of nine years, tried to look very manly as he planted a kiss on his grandfather's cheek. They all loved the grandpa who fed them bananas with honey, swung them high as he picked them up, and gave them a bath with the hand shower tickling them. "Shall we all sing 'He Was A Jolly Good Fellow' for grandpa?" I suggested, and we sang full throated, each in a different pitch, trying to outdo the other. "Granny, can we also say 'hip, hip, hurray' for grandpa?" asked Nikta. They all piped up with three cheers.

I explained that many people would be coming by to say good-bye to grandpa and asked them to play quietly in the guest room until it was time to send grandpa on his final journey. The children somberly filed out of the room just as the doctor arrived to officially pronounce Sri dead. I planted a kiss on Sri's forehead. His body was cold. I wiped the tear that had fallen from my eye to the bridge of his nose. I wanted to see him off in his naval uniform and had prepared it for him. I had also typed out the announcement for the papers and prepared the photograph. In the photo he looked so happy, with that disarming smile of his. That was what attracted me to him when I was escorted to his house by my parents forty years ago, so he could propose to me properly. I watched while Arjun and Anil stood by their father. He looked so serene, his hands crossed on his chest. People had started to arrive, Sri's siblings, cousins, aunts and uncles. "Are you afraid of death?" I had quizzed Sri. "No," he said without hesitation. "I am afraid of disability." "Aunty," whispered Susan. "Do you want to change your dress?" Sri liked to see me in a saree and I wanted to bid farewell to him wearing one. As I dressed, I missed the whistle of appreciation he would always greet me with when I wore a saree. I saw my face in the mirror and wondered how I would look without a *Bindi* dot on my forehead. If I had died first, would Sri have stopped wearing a tie? No, so I would continue to wear my *bindi* to honor Sri.

We placed a garland of Marigold on Sri's body and it looked so attractive against his white uniform. Someone placed a garland of jasmine flowers on the Marigold, and I could hear the priest telling me it was time to call the family to place more flowers. The grandchildren and I each placed a garland and kissed his cheek. The flowers looked very much like they did when I had placed garlands on him at our wedding. But that was different. There was loud and happy music, everyone wore gold bordered sarees, I was dressed as a bride and he had that naughty smile in his eyes. Now the priest recited mantras and Sri had his eyes closed. In fact, he did not have his eyes. An eye donation team had taken them away. They were a very good pair of eyes and someone else would see through them now. There was no music and all who had assembled looked sad and wore drab clothes. The priest said that he was a good man who fulfilled his duties towards his parents, wife, children, grandchildren and also to his country.

Sri was lifted on a stretcher and it was as if they were taking away part of me. Then he was gone, like so many millions before him. Death is not a unique experience, it is universal. Yet when it touches someone you love, why does it feel like it is happening only to you? That was the last time I would see him and touch him. I had heard his voice and felt his breath for the last time.

After everything had been attended to, the house was so quiet. I sat on the bed and put my hand on his pillow. I would sleep alone now. Sri was not there to snuggle up with. The marital couch was not just a platform for physical pleasure, it was a real haven for me. In years past, I had often put my head on his shoulder and told him all of the day's escapades. He would gently stroke my arm and if his stroking stopped, I would ask, "Are you listening?" And he would continue, to signal that he was and that I could feel secure. The bed looked so big.

I closed my eyes and felt calm again. I was alone, but I would not be lonely. I had memories to cherish of him right up until the end of our time together. Even in the confusion at the end of his life, there had been a special moment when he had looked up into my eyes as I was wiping his face and had said, "I am lucky to have a mother like you." I also had been lucky to share what we had lived, together.

Power of Prayer
: Chapter Five

PRAYER IS SIMPLY COMMUNICATING WITH GOD, and so, of course, there is no wrong or right way to pray. Your prayer is unique to you and can be held quietly in your heart and made in your thoughts, or be spoken, danced or sung. To find your own path to prayer begin with what feels most authentic to you and experiment with how prayer can be a daily part of your life.

If you memorized a prayer in childhood you can start there. *Four corners round my bed, four angels round my head. One to watch, two to pray, and one to chase bad things away.* Simply begin praying, and then keep talking to God. You can find grace every day when the lines of communication are open.

I find the most meaningful kind of prayer to be a prayer of gratitude. Before you ask for anything, make it clear to your Creator that you know what you are grateful for and give thanks for all that you have. This daily checking in with God can be your lifeline when you make it a regular part of each day. Find wonderful places to pray, find creative ways to pray, and develop the habit of prayer. Become so used to praying daily that on those rare occasions when you forget to pray you will feel how much you miss it and return to prayer again with eagerness.

Prayer Works

A year ago, after a big event I organized, a group of women decided we would meet once a month to speak about spiritual things and to encourage each other to grow and change. We found ourselves returning to the subject of prayer again and again. We grew in faith, we attended to our spiritual lives with intention, and we explored many ways to pray. We wanted to know if prayer worked, how it worked, and why.

I grew up in a praying family, and in the past few years in particular, I have seen that prayer needs to be such a natural part of life that God is a partner in times of crisis, in times of celebration, and in the small details of life. I know how important it is to invite God into our every day concerns. Minister Mary Edwards remembers a day years ago, when she learned an important lesson about how to handle money, and when prayer made a difference.

I think of it as the day the wind stood still. When I discovered that all of the money my husband and I had was missing, I was panic-stricken. I'm telling you there were enough beads of perspiration on my forehead to string a 24-inch necklace. My empty hand, which I had just taken out of my pocket, trembled uncontrollably.

I had developed a bad habit of stuffing money into my pocket instead of placing it carefully into my purse. Now, I was suffering the consequences of my carelessness, and the money we needed for groceries for the week was gone.

Between the house and the supermarket, where I now stood, the money could have fallen out of my pocket almost anywhere. Company was coming for dinner that evening; we needed food to carry us to the next check, and the money was gone. How could I explain my carelessness to my husband?

Retracing my steps, I returned to the post office where I had dropped off several mailbags. I had just completed a mailing for our ministry of five thousand pieces of mail. Could the money have fallen into one of the mailbags? When the postal clerk said, "Lady, as high as the wind is today, that money is long gone by now." It was hard to choke back the tears. The wind really is high, I thought to myself in despair.

I returned to my office where I had worked that morning. As I traced my steps through the building, one of my co-workers joined the search. The money was nowhere to be found. "Will you pray with me? I've got to find the money." I said to my colleague. We prayed together and I left for my next destination. When I got in my car I couldn't hold back the tears any longer. They broke open like a floodgate. In between the sobs I cried out to the Lord, "Father, I'm so scared. Forgive me for my carelessness. I have learned a lesson from this experience. I will be careful with money from now on. Wherever the money is, please surround it with angels." I sensed the peace of God enter into my heart and heard Him instruct me to go home.

As I turned into my driveway, I could see it. The money had fallen on my neighbor's lawn. I heard a voice say, "Look around." This I what I saw: the mailman had just delivered mail to my next-door neighbor and he didn't see the money on the lawn, children were playing nearby, and they didn't see it, dogs were barking and roaming the street, and they hadn't noticed the money. And, yes, the wind was still high and yet in four hours it hadn't blown the money away.

Do I believe in repentance? You bet I do. I don't believe that my money would have been there for me had I not repented of my carelessness. Do I believe in the power of prayer? Yes, I do. Did I learn a lesson? You bet I did. Do I believe in everyday miracles? Absolutely.

Asking for Confirmation

Growing up in the countryside in Jamaica, we traveled for miles on dirt roads. There were no street signs. There were no numbers on the gates – there were no gates. If you wanted to know where someone lived, you simply asked for them and people in the village would point the way. We lived in the house on a small hill next to the church. There was running water in our house, but it came from a big tank in our yard and we had no electricity. We used an oil lamp for light. There were no doctors and there was no pharmacy where I lived.

Late one night, when I was about twelve years old, my father suddenly became deathly ill. We did not have a phone and we did not have a car, so we could not take my father to the hospital, which was an hour's drive away. All we could do was pray. I cried out to God to heal my father. I prayed with everything I had in me.

Over the years, I thought I remembered that my father had gotten better right there and then, and that he felt my prayers had healed him. My family hadn't spoken about that night for years, and over time I thought that perhaps my memory was incorrect. Just a few years ago, during a painful time when I was questioning the power of prayer, I thought of that night, but I didn't have the courage to ask my family what they remembered. Of course, I got the answer I needed in a casual conversation with my brother, the Reverend Wayne Vernon, who brought up what had happened that night and described my prayers as healing our father. My sister Veronica spoke to me about the same night in another unrelated conversation. Out of the blue, she asked me if I remembered the time our father was so sick and we all felt sure he was dying. She said, "You prayed for him, Lorna, and he was healed."

I needed the confirmation that prayers could be answered. I needed the reassurance that I could believe in the power of prayer and God provided it.

I had been praying and crying out to God to help me change my life and things seemed to be getting worse. I was at a very low point but I continued praying, hoping to find the faith. God's time was different from my time, and God had better ideas than I did about my life. When I pray and tell God my ideas now, I ask for "this or something better," knowing that He will show the way.

The Power Of Group Prayer

My first memory of group prayer was with the women in my church in Jamaica, who would gather together at someone's home for prayer and fasting. They had been doing this for years. Sometimes, I would have the privilege of attending and together we would sing hymns and pray all day. When a good fasting and praying time was underway, the word spread and strangers would come from a far distance, walking miles to come to the home of someone they did not know to ask the group to offer a specific prayer.

In group prayer, we would sing hymns for hours and read and discuss a particular Bible verse. But most of all, we opened up our hearts and prayed for many hours. As the years went by, some of the people who had received answers to their prayer emigrated, leaving Jamaica usually for England, the United States, or Canada. Often these people didn't want to lose touch with the prayer group and so would send their prayers by mail.

I truly believe in the power of group prayer because I've felt it. I encourage you to try putting your prayer requests in the box at church, or making a request for prayer over the Internet. Join a prayer group and feel the power of prayer magnified. There are prayers groups all over the world who join together to unify their voices and their hearts. Imagine what the world could be, if all of God's children prayed and asked for grace and everyday miracles.

Johnese Burtram knows that the prayers of many comforted her family in a time of crisis. She also believes that these prayers helped save the life of her baby. Her faith in the power of prayer and the courage she exhibited in surrendering to God's will remind us of the courage it takes to face the worst of times.

Something was definitely wrong with my baby. I knew it as soon as I finished nursing him. "Honey, I think Josh is getting sick," I worried as I walked my husband to the door that May morning. "His temperature seems pretty high and he threw up everything right after I fed him."

"He has a doctor's appointment tomorrow, right?"
"Yeah. I'll see how the day goes and I'll call you."

Josh and I kissed Daddy goodbye at the front door. As I closed the door Joshua went into convulsions in my arms. I had heard about infant convulsions, but this was terrifying. His eyes rolled back, his little head fell back and his body jerked violently. "Oh, Jesus, this is serious. Please help us," I prayed anxiously.

I was so scared. Frantically, I opened the door, just in time to see Ken's car turn the corner and disappear. I was home with my five year-old and his two year-old brother. I called the rescue squad, breathless and in tears, my words almost incoherent. I could hardly tell them where I lived. Then I called Ken's office. "Sylvia!" I begged Ken's secretary. "Josh is really sick. He has a high fever and he went into convulsions and help is coming. I couldn't stop Ken. He needs to come back home." Bless her heart. She not only deciphered my message and sent my husband home, more importantly, she started the prayer network in our church family.

Josh's convulsions had subsided but he was extremely hot. Waiting for help, I prayed constantly as I cuddled my sick baby. My mind raced with so many tragic scenarios. And the worst was what would have happened if I had put him down after his feeding for his usual nap and wasn't there to see the convulsions. What might have been seemed even worse than what was, and that was bad enough.

The EMTs arrived and shortly after that so did my husband. Josh's temperature was over 106_ degrees. Ken accompanied Joshua in the ambulance, while I followed in the car with our other boys.

At the hospital, the emergency room pediatrician took one look at Joshua and exclaimed, "This is a very sick baby."

I sympathized with Joshua's piteous cries as they immersed him in tepid water to lower his temperature. "Mama's so sorry you're sick, baby boy," I crooned softly. "Don't worry. Jesus is watching over you."

A spinal tap confirmed spinal meningitis. Josh would have to be admitted to isolation immediately until a spinal fluid culture confirmed the type of meningitis he had contracted. Before admitting him, they allowed me to nurse him one more time. Miraculously, he did not throw up this feeding, which was the last one he would have for three days. Ken and I clung to each other as they took our baby, hooked him up to numerous IVs and monitors, and placed him in isolation.

The vigil began and ministry colleagues came to pray with us. Late in the evening, Ken went to be with our four other children at their grandparents' house and I sat with Joshua. That first night, I watched the expanding soft spot in Josh's head. He looked like he had a pointed head. A parade of nurses and doctors came through, explaining the swelling was caused by the infection of the meninges and spinal fluid. The swelling around the brain was not only dangerous, but very painful. The intravenous medications were to reduce the swelling, manage the pain, and fight the infection. Were they using the right antibiotic? That question could only be answered with the results of the spinal fluid culture. IV machines beeped and monitors ticked away through the long night, sending out their ominous-sounding reports. It was an exceedingly frightening night.

As I cradled six month old Joshua, I prayed with a desperate single focus. Powerless, I was acutely aware that this situation was beyond my control. For the first time ever, I could do nothing to help my child. Everything in my repertoire of mothering skills was helplessly inadequate.

I cried out for God's mercy and also knew that Joshua belonged to God and that his life was in God's hands.

Through the night, my little one slept fitfully as I held him, tenaciously praying to hold my ground. I thought of a verse in I Corinthians, "Stand firm. Let nothing move you." God granted the petitions of the many prayers that assailed heaven that night. Our son survived those critical first hours.

The spinal fluid-culture identified the strain of meningitis. It was a type that was usually fatal but Josh became the "miracle baby" of the pediatric ward. The entire ward was abuzz with the news of his remarkable progress. During his ten days in isolation, his amazing recovery gave us many opportunities to witness to God's faithfulness and healing grace. Joshua recovered completely with no adverse effects.

Josh will soon be twenty-one and is a third year theology major at a Christian college. Our lives are determined by Divine Providence and our prayers connect us to a loving God.

Trusting God's Plan

Recently, I received an e-mail message from a friend who asked me to pray for her sister who was very ill and in intensive care. My friend asked that her sister be healed. The sister seemed to be doing better for a time and then several weeks later, I received an e-mail message from my friend passing along the news that her sister had just died.

I have such faith in prayer, that I thought because we had prayed for her, she would be healed and have a full recovery. I learned from my friend that God's definition of what it means to be healed was a very beautiful thing. My friend explained that, at the end, her sister had changed and was healed and whole in spirit, and that she had been ready to die with grace and in peace. Once again, I understood that as we pray, we are to accept the outcome and trust in God.

A Sign From God

This story from Lynne Cooper Sitton will bring a smile of recognition as you remember the times you've asked for a sign, and gotten answers that were so loud and clear it seemed as if God wanted to make sure you didn't miss the point.

"I hate for you to spend so much time working in that kitchen and have it be so unpleasant!" my mother said on the phone. "At least get an estimate for a renovation." Oh! How we needed a new kitchen. My twenty-five year old appliances and countertops were beyond shot. My husband and I hosted at least fifteen people for weekly Bible study meeting in the kitchen and occasionally we held potluck suppers as well. The stovetop and the dishwasher desperately needed repairs or re-placement, and the dishwasher door opened directly in front of the sink, making it practically impossible to load or unload. If we replaced the "modern inconvenience" and relocated the new dishwasher to a logical place, new countertops would be required. With a new dishwasher and new countertops, the trashed cupboards wouldn't make any sense. And the old gas wall oven was probably dangerous. "At least an estimate," She encouraged. "Okay, Mom," I sighed, knowing my husband Bob would not consider these expenditures right now.

We expected a transfer in the coming year, so patch it up and move on was his military mentality. Still, it wouldn't hurt to get an estimate for redoing an unsafe, inefficient, and outdated kitchen. Real estate agents always said that bathroom and kitchen upgrades increased the value of a property. I whispered an absentminded prayer, "Lord, You'll have to show Bob the way, if You want this to happen."

As I had predicted, my husband dismissed the idea of any major renova-tions, and laughed out loud when I presented him with the proposed estimate for a kitchen remodel. But within a few days, some odd things began to happen. A stranger phoned, asking if we wanted to sell our kitchen cabinets. He had heard we might be getting rid of ours. Puzzled, I assured him I'd call back if we did. A Sunday comic strip poked fun at a husband who had just bought new office equipment, but didn't want to buy a new stove. "That's different! I work there!" the caption explained. Finally, a neighbor called to report that the fire department had just left a home on her street where a gas oven just like ours had exploded and burned the kitchen. The insulation of the oven had deteriorated and it was like a ticking time bomb. My neighbor said, "Maybe God is trying to save you from a fire."

None of these little "divine signs" made any impact on Bob. He shrugged and said, "Sweetheart, the Lord will just have to show me that it's alright for us to spend money on a new kitchen. So many people are starving in this world. I need be sure that we are good stewards of what the Lord has given us." I figured I'd be struggling in that kitchen 'til the cows came home, so I dropped the subject, waiting to see if the Lord would send any more signs.

When the carpenter mentioned he needed a decision and a down payment on the new cabinets if we were going ahead with the project, I laughed. "Don't hold your breath!" I joked. "Bob needs God to hit him upside the head with a sign for us to do this! But we'll give you a definite answer on Monday."

Friday dawned sunny and warm and we headed to a church retreat in the beautiful Shenandoah Mountains for a weekend of family fun and spiritual renewal. We made a quick stop at the church so Bob could drop off some Sunday-school material on the youth pastor's desk, and then we were off. Bob and I chatted and listened to favorite Christian music, while our little boy, Jay, rode in the back of the station wagon. We anticipated a terrific weekend together. Suddenly, the sunshine disappeared and raindrops dotted the windshield. "Jay," Bob called out, above the music, "Do you see any rainbows back there?"

"There's one!" I interjected, pointing to a huge white billboard with a fifteen-foot red, yellow and blue rainbow emblazoned across the top and big black letters announcing *Auntie Em's Kitchen.* Bob's face glowed beet red and his hands gripped the steering wheel, his knuckles turning ghostly white. "What's wrong, Hon? Are you okay?" I asked.
"Well, yes. I guess we're getting a new kitchen," he said.
"What?" I stammered, surprised at his about-face on the issue.
"Yeah," Bob looked at me in amused confusion. "This morning, when

I was praying, I asked the Lord to give me a sign if we were supposed to do the kitchen renovation. I told Him I'd look for a rainbow. A rainbow was good enough for Noah, so it was fine for me. When we stopped at church and I went into the pastor's office, there was a book on his desk with a rainbow on the cover. "I told the Lord, 'No! No substitutes for the real thing.' Then I turned to leave, and saw a big picture of a rainbow on the office wall. Again, I told the Lord I wanted a real rainbow as a sign. Now, instead of a sign, He has given me a gigantic rainbow on a billboard about a kitchen. I can't miss that. Order the cabinets. God wants us to have a new kitchen!"

In the next couple of months, our outdated and unsafe kitchen was transformed into the lovely, efficient center of our home. Bob's military transfer was local, so we didn't have to relocate and we stayed in our house for another three years. We continued to host the weekly Bible study group. And every time we entertained, I gave thanks for those new appliances and the expansive new countertops. I rejoiced in the peaceful, attractive environment that welcomed so many to our "kitchen ministry" for mentoring, prayer, or Godly counsel. Because of those renovations, we even gave a wedding reception for a group member. Like Gideon in the Bible (Judges 6: 36-40), the Lord guided Bob with a sign – a really big sign!

Ask and it shall be given. But we do need to ask. And if the asking is new to you, remember that the more you pray the more sure you will feel in your connection to God. Your prayers can be simple, they can be long, they can take many forms, and the answers can also come in many ways and through many signs.

Here is a simple prayer I pray daily. It helps me know that all is well. *Dear God, thank you for loving me so. Please help me to be a blessing to someone today. Amen.* These are simple words but that's all we need with God. All we need is a sincere heart and a yearning to connect with the Divine. One of the simplest prayers we know is found in the twenty-third psalm, it's just fifteen simple lines known by many people around the world. Find your simple words and your way to connect with God.

Read this story by Amy Wiley in silence.

Celebration of Life

I awakened to the usual noise of plastic crinkling. Mom was stumbling sleepily downstairs to warm the bag of sugar water used in her kidney dialysis. I rolled out of bed, yawning, and hurried to get ready for the day. That night we were throwing a baby shower for my oldest sister, Angela.

Angela's baby would be the first grandchild in the family. The shower had grown to a huge affair–up to forty women were expected! But a shadow lay over the house. Mom's dialysis was no longer working effectively and deadly toxins were once more building up in her body.

Yet through this trial and many others over the last few years, including seven surgeries, my mom had stayed faithful. Scheduled around her four daily dialysis exchanges, she continued to serve in the church, help at homeschool events, mentor young mothers, and teach me my senior year of high school. But most of all she continued to praise God for the blessings she found among the troubles. The doctors were astonished at her energy and spirits.

We knew that God could touch her and heal her at any moment. But I also knew that this was not His plan for us. I could see the impact her faith had on doctors, friends, even a lady in the grocery store. And so we waited, praying for His healing through the doctors' hands.

Unknown to us, there were others praying that very morning. Even as I climbed into the shower, one woman was kneeling by her bed, "Lord, give Carol a kidney–today." And as I brushed out my long hair my cousin was pleading, "Heal Aunt Carol, Lord. Bring her a transplant soon."

Medically-speaking, a transplant was not something that would happen that day or any day soon. The average wait for a kidney transplant through the national donor list was two years. Mom had been on the list for only six months.

That evening I came in as Mom was mopping the kitchen floor. She was breathing heavily and her yellowed skin looked even more sickly in the evening light. "I'll finish," I told her, taking the mop as the phone rang. Mom answered it and I froze as I listened to the one-sided conversation. Surely it couldn't be what it sounded like!

She hung up the phone. "That was OHSU," she whispered. "They have a kidney that matches me and we have to be to the hospital within two hours."

I laughed and cried at the same time. Suddenly mopping the floor seemed like an odd thing to be doing and I set down the mop, running to get the rest of the family. We went into high gear, packing Mom's bags for the hospital stay and calling friends.

Just as we were leaving, Angela arrived for her baby shower. "We're headed to OHSU!" we hollered out the car window. "Are you coming or staying?" She stared at us in shock as we explained delightedly, "Mom's getting a kidney!"

She gasped. "Well, I –, I guess I better stay here since forty women are coming for my shower. I'll come over after the party. Bye!" She grinned and waved as we sped down the driveway.

Meanwhile, the women began arriving at our house. Each guest was greeted at the door with the wonderful news of their answered prayers. What a blessing to have forty women gathered at our house to pray as the transplant process began. A party for one new life suddenly turned into a party for two "new" lives!

We reached the hospital and the rigorous tests began to ensure that Mom's body was healthy enough to handle a transplant. At one point, four different doctors were nearly banging heads as they all tried to look into her mouth at the same time. They were particularly concerned about her sore tooth, because the surgery could not be done if she had any sign of infection in her body.

Finally the doctors announced, "Everything looks fine. We'll do the transplant first thing in the morning." Mom didn't stop grinning until the anesthesia kicked in the next day.

Early the next morning as Mom was wheeled toward surgery, a nurse plopped a cardboard box on her gurney. "There it is! Bond." Surprised, we saw that the box was marked, 'Right Kidney'. "What are you going to name it?" the nurse asked.

"Fast Working," Mom announced. Perhaps it was a prophecy--to the doctors' astonishment, the kidney began working on the operating table.

One month later Mom was sitting in a hospital once again. This time her skin was pink and healthy and in her arms lay her new grand-daughter, a child she would live to see grow up to love the God who answers prayer.

Making the Connection

WE EITHER HAVE A CONNECTION TO GOD or we don't. We live in a world where many people think money or fame can fix anything and everything, but looking to these things for happiness causes people to lose a connection to their authentic self and to God. We need to look in the mirror and ask ourselves, "Do I have a connection with God?"

How do you connect with God, and is what you are currently doing working for you? Some people move from church to church, from a mega church to a small church, from one branch of a faith to another. I know people who go to two churches in the same day. We do yoga, we meditate, and we pray together and alone. Anything can work, if we have a sincere desire to connect. Don't worry about waiting until you feel better. God accepts us as we are, broken or whole.

We can investigate our past, we can dream about our future, and the most challenging thing we can do is to stay in the moment and find God there. There is no place in the world where God cannot be found. Look for him everywhere. God lives in our hearts and in what we do to help our brothers and sisters. This is how we show God that we see him in others, by treating people kindly.

Finding Strength Within

Making the connection with God is an inside job, and when it happens we find great strength. When we connect with God, we develop a boldness that can surprise us. Imagine getting up in the morning full of energy, feeling unstoppable, and knowing that life is full of grace and goodness. Relying on the Holy Spirit allows us to see light in even the worst situations, and helps us make better choices. We can put our past and our failings in perspective, live fully in the moment, and know that our future is linked to God's will. With God, we can find strength even in the darkest of times. Lakisha Mcclendon shares her journey from darkness to light in this harrowing story of survival.

Twenty-one years ago my life changed very quickly. It was a beautiful day in November and I was playing with my siblings out in the yard with our Big Wheels like we always did on a day like this. As the sun began to set, my mother prepared us for bed. This was the last time my mother would ever kiss her children goodnight.

In the middle of the night as we slept, my stepfather decided that he just could not see life as it was continuing, and so he shot my mother and then turned the .38 caliber handgun on himself. None of us saw it coming. And decades later, I would find that I had fallen into a situation that was very similar, without seeing it coming either.

I was twenty-one years old when I met the man who would become my youngest son's father. He was everything I wanted in a man. He was humorous, good-looking, street-smart, and he had some money. After a few months of dating him, he had me right where he wanted me. I was in love with him.

At this point, things started spiraling out of control and he made the demands and pulled the strings. The violence began slowly, and, at first, I didn't realize I was in a dangerous situation. Each day I prayed for God to change this man, to make him into the person that I had loved so much. After praying for four and a half years, things were only getting worse and I realized that I needed to pray to change myself. I tried to calm him during his rages, and I tried to do everything he demanded of me so that I would not end up dead like my mother.

I prayed for God to make me stronger, I needed the courage to leave him, but I also knew it might even be more dangerous to pack up my bags, grabs my kids, and go. I still loved him and I still had the hope that he could change until Christmas night of 2004. I wondered why God had dealt me this hand. I felt I was meant to fail. I was trying, but I felt like I was losing the battle and then I experienced the darkest night of my life.

The day had been relatively peaceful. The kids had unwrapped their
gifts, family had come and gone, we had played music together and had
enjoyed each other as a family. Later that night, he insisted that I come
with him to a party at the home of a woman he had carried on an affair
with for a year during our relationship. When I said I wouldn't go with
him, he raged and screamed obscenities at me. He was shaking uncontrollably, he was so angry. I was afraid of him and so I suggested he go
alone. He called a woman he had also had relations with during the time
we were together to ask her to go to the party with him. My heart felt
like it was literally being ripped out of my chest and I knew I had finally
had enough.

I told him that if he went, I would leave him and not come back. His
hands wrapped tightly around my neck and I begged for my life. He
cried as he choked me, asking me why I was making him do this to me.
He said he loved me and could not be without me. The thought of my
kids growing up without a mother, like I had, flashed before me. And I
knew then that dying was not an option, so I fought back. I managed
to break away from his choke hold and I started throwing punches and
anything else I could put my hands on. When he caught me, he hit me
like I was nothing more than a punching bag. He beat me until I could
not move anymore. He said he was sorry and that he loved me. I turned
away because I knew that he could not possibly love me and treat me
like that. The price for turning away was high. He violently raped me, as
he had in the past, but this time I was so injured the pain was incredible. I begged and pleaded for him not to; I was so bruised and broken.
I held on to consciousness knowing that when it was over, he would
sleep, and I could figure out a way to break this cycle. I had to live for
my kids and I had to get out of there.

Later, I eased my body off of the bed and away from him. I slowly
walked towards the bathroom to take a look at myself. As I saw what he
had done to me, the fire begin to burn deep down within my soul
as I examined every wound, every bruise, and all of my previous scars.
I began to pray. I asked God to forgive me for my sins. I prayed that
my kids would understand. I prayed that my kids wouldn't grow up to
be like him. I prayed that we could leave safely. I prayed that night like

I never had before. I prayed myself right into salvation. It was on that night that I started to really believe that God would not give up on me and that there was hope. He was waiting for me to call on him and I did and my life was changed.

I have talked to many men and women who say they continue to make the same mistake over and over. My sense is that, when we do this, we need extra help from God to break the cycle that holds us. We need that connection with God to be so strong that we can break free of the chains of our bad habits, our old patterns, and our limited ways of seeing things. I also think we need to be compassionate and not be so quick to judge ourselves. Forgiveness and freedom come from God, and our direct connection to God. If we can feel that connection, we can learn and grow. If we draw close to God we can become free of our mistakes and can get past our old limitations.

Seeing Others As God Does

Learning to love others more completely is another way we are able make the connection with God. Love comes from a space that is pure. Love allows us to see others as God would have us see them. We can practice the golden rule and try hard to love others as we love ourselves. Just imagine the peace we can experience when we love in this way.

To love the way God loves means to practice love freely. We cannot pick and choose who to love. We are told we must love everyone and that this is the great commandment. The light of God will start to shine through when we focus on this teaching. We will know who we really are. We will be able to connect to our birthright; we will connect to our source.

God also tells us to become as little children. This doesn't give us permission to be childish; it is an encouragement to be open to seeing the beauty and simplicity of God in everything. Look at children as God does and then see how you can be as clear and open as a child. When we feel God's presence everywhere, we learn to trust. Trusting that God will take care of us, we learn not to judge ourselves or others and are free to be more deeply connected to God. When I'm working with someone who needs to become more like a child, I encourage them to schedule a play day where they can empty their mind of all the cares of the world and trust God. This is a way to rediscover joy.

Without Limitation

To make the connection with God, we need to center our thoughts on things that are larger and more eternal than our present circumstances. We must come to understanding that in God we have all that we need. If we invest our best attention in feelings of lack and limitation, at the end of the day we will find lack and limitation. If we draw from the Divine Source, we will experience fullness and a sense of completion and wholeness. Tap God as the source of your life and your cup will run over.

I talked to someone recently who felt a sense of calling about a new direction in his life. We agreed that once God gives you your marching orders, there is no need to go to a committee for approval. Usually, we go to the committee in our own head first. We sit down with all the parts of us who jump in to remind us about our limitations, tell us that we have failed before and that we will fail again, and say the things that flatten our dreams. God's direction is more compelling and more real than the committee we hear in our heads. Sometimes, at a crossroads, we check in with a second committee made up of family and friends. Of course, they always have advice for us, and although some of it may be wise and loving, some of their advice may only serve to remind us of our limitations, encourage us to start small, or not at all. People project their own fears onto others all the time, and even when people feel they are being realistic and helpful, there may be more going on under the surface.

When we connect with God, we can trust the loving pull we feel to be true to ourselves and to be more Godly. There are no buried motives and there is no lack of clarity when we connect with God through an open heart. Follow the direction you feel comes from God and your limitations will fall away. Diane Pitts has a wonderful story to share about how she was able to move from a sense of limitation to a more expansive life. She lived through a special time that showed her that all things are possible.

It was Monday already and my head was pounding. "What if I'm making a mistake?" I whined to my husband for the hundredth time. I flopped into my chair at the breakfast table and admitted all my fears to him.

"It will be fine," Darrell encouraged. On his way out the door, he chuckled and added," Besides, it's too late to turn back now. You committed to be there."

After five years of being away from my career as a physical therapist, I felt strongly that it was time to return. My husband was supportive and various circumstances paved the way. My heart longed for it, but still I was unsure of myself. Gripping my coffee cup, I tried to gain courage from the warmth. Then a phrase came to my mind. *Without me you can do nothing, but with me all things are possible.* Was thinking this thought a sign of God's assurance and grace? I jotted the phrase on a note pad and repeated it. Savoring the last of my coffee, I checked my e-mail on the way to get my lab coat. The daily devotional I received reminded me that a goal from God could not be blocked. Nothing could keep me from being what He called me to be. There it was again. *All things are possible.*

I piled into the car with our three boys and an onslaught commenced. "Mom, what are we going to do?" Jacob moaned.
"Are you going to be working all the time?" asked Tyler.
"When are you coming home?" John whined. The voices of my three boys chimed together in a barrage of questions that had already been answered. Guilty Mom Syndrome closed in with relentless force. The things the boys said mirrored my own insecurities. They weren't hiding their fear, and I was masking mine. "Guys, I'm not going to be gone all the time. Only two days this week. You're staying with Linda, and I'll see you by five o'clock. We have to try it and see if it works." By the time I dropped the boys off, my nerves felt raw but my mind held onto the hope that I would be adequate and up to the task.

At the hospital, I took a deep breath and after a few hours of orientation, I began working with patients again. I felt great, but could I still make a difference? I looked at my assignment. The patient information read: Room 1220, diagnosis of Immune Deficiency, Rheumatoid Arthritis . Opening the door, I saw a shriveled youngster who looked like an old man. Family members hovered nearby with wary expressions. The patient stared blankly at the wall. His father urged him to look at me, but his gaze was vacant as if he was saying, *I have too many problems. Everybody else has given up. Why bother?* Looking for common ground, I glanced around the room and spotted a balloon. It read, *With God all things are possible.* How strange to see those words! Did this boy believe it? Did I?

"Would you like for me to pray with you?" I whispered, as he grimaced in pain. He nodded that he would. In a few minutes, the young man was moving painful limbs and attempting to help himself for the first time in two weeks. In his eyes I now saw a willingness to try, an attempt to believe, even when it really didn't seem worthwhile. His unspoken trust urged me to attempt what others might deem a waste of time. And even though his disease had weakened his reserves, this boy was valuable and God cherished him enough to send a rusty therapist to a hospital room to reassure him that he mattered. In return, God was telling me, his therapist, that through this helpless boy I could see that *all things are possible.*

The day sped by. I tried not to be insecure but focused on what I knew to be true. I listened not to self-doubt, but to the voice that assured me I was in the right place. *You will learn the new computer system. You can make new friends. Your skills are still useful. You can make a difference.* Before I knew it, the day was over. I couldn't get the appreciation I had seen in the boy's eyes or the unusual balloon out of my mind. When I stopped to pick up the children, Linda asked me in for coffee. She offered me an attractive mug. "It's new, isn't it?" I remarked. Linda showed me the details of the garden gate on the mug. She said she liked to think of it as an invitation to a new adventure. I started to take a sip but froze when I spotted the words printed inside the rim. *All things are possible.* Through the eyes of a boy and in the words of God that were turning up all around me, I was finding that indeed, all things are possible.

His Presence

When we connect with God, we touch into the vastness and feel the infinite stretching before us. We feel what is truly possible. Our job is to make the connection and then turn the details over to God. We can also feel his presence without forcing the connection. We can simply go with the flow and let God's presence fill us up in his own time. As Ann FitzHenry explains, the joy is in the journey.

Rainbow, mommy, rainbow!" Glancing up at the sky with a quick, "That's nice, honey." I finally did slow down and stop. A majestic double rainbow illuminated the mist with a vibrant spectrum of light. Blazing across the morning sky, the arc of the rainbow hugged the horizon. The ends, just out of reach, touched the ground with radiant splendor. I was filled with reverence. God's beauty stretched like a banner before us. Time stopped as we marveled at the iridescent colors suspended in the atmosphere. Our earthly obligations seemed to vanish, as we stood transfixed staring at the heavens. For several awestruck minutes, we rejoiced in God's reassurance that His hand holds all of our tomorrows.

With our thoughts in the stratosphere, we piled into the car, saying good-bye to the rainbow. Driving through our neighborhood, we encountered women in housecoats and men with morning newspapers all staring up at the sky. Several people clutched cameras trying to capture the rainbow's brilliance. The crossing guard smiled and made an arc with his fingers. Two thumbs up was our enthusiastic reply.

In the guise of an ordinary morning, we had been reminded of God's profound presence in the world. For a lovely moment, we were a community of believers rejoicing in the early morning sunlight. While much of the city slept, a few of us had shared the gift. The hustle and bustle of life slowed for a few minutes and in a world where there was never enough time for kissing toy lizards and playing in sandboxes, God gave us a chance to consider what was really important. In the still dawn of an April morning, we had shared His joy as we looked up at the heavens.

True Self
: Chapter Seven

KNOWING WHAT GOD HAS IN MIND for us can take some time, but finding our most authentic self is worth the effort. A few years ago, I was getting close to knowing my true self and understanding the totality of the work I needed to do. I felt I was getting closer to understanding what God wanted from me, but I needed some help to come the final distance.

During this time in my life, I had answered the call to work with professional women and to inspire them to live a more balanced life. I knew I had something to offer in bringing mind, body, and spirit together, and I felt I could help lead the kind of change that I had undertaken in my own life. But my total vision at the time was to be a motivational speaker – and I wasn't even mentioning the most important aspect of motivation in my presentation. I did not reference my personal walk with God when I talked to women about their full empowerment. I thought my spiritual life needed to be separate from my professional life. But the workshops I was leading at the time weren't sustaining me financially, so I prayed to understand how I could be more successful at my professional mission. I felt that a relationship with God was critical to my own success, but I was intentionally keeping God out of my work with other women.

Late one night, I was so worried that I wouldn't be able to make it financially that I cried out to God, praying earnestly, "Who am I and what do you want from me?" I had a strong feeling that the Holy Spirit was telling me that I was on the right track, but I felt the encouragement to go much deeper. I had a sense that I was supposed to minister to people, but I had rejected that idea for a long time because I thought it was the last thing I wanted to do.

My father was a deacon in a church and my parents started a church in our living room in Jamaica. My brother serves as the pastor of a Word of Life Worship Center in a thriving church in Old Habour, Jamaica. I love my background as the daughter of a preacher. I appreciate the life foundation that knowing the Bible and praying has given me. My belief in God is unshakable. Still, I had decided early in my life that I did not want to be a minister and I had been stubbornly sticking to that idea.

In my dark night of the soul, it came to me that I was already a minister, and that my personal struggle was part of my growth and development – both as a person and as a professional woman. I had been in a dark valley, but in that process I was learning the tools I needed to attend to myself and to support women in their professional and personal growth. Then and there, I decided to change the name of the meetings I was holding in order to conform more closely to what I now understood God wanted me to do. My workshops became the Women Spirituality Series. As I made this decision, I heard the Holy Spirit whisper inside me, *Do this and women will join you.*

The women who attend the monthly meeting are faithful and strong. We meet at the Ritz Carlton Hotel in Coconut Grove, Miami. I believe it is important for us to be surrounded with beauty in order to inspire our largest lives, and so we enjoy meeting in a room overlooking the marina with lovely sofas stacked high with colorful pillows or in a comfortable room with an exquisite fireplace. There are always roses in the room and scented candles burning because I believe this helps set a mood for tuning into our highest nature and healing and growing together.

Tuning Into Your True Self

When we are surrounded by love and beauty, we can more easily tune into our true self. The abundance that surrounds us can be brought into our hearts as we embrace who we really are and face the potential of what we can become. Prosperity is a mind-set, and money and success of every kind flows from feeling comfortable with abundance and welcoming it. Together, we can make miracles happen when we gather in beautiful settings to connect with who we are most authentically. When I envision what happens next with this work, I see the vision of this kind of gathering spreading around the world so that thousands of us can inspire and encourage each other. I see us gathering in Jamaica and other beautiful places. I see us sharing our stories and changing our lives. I see us gathering in groups large enough that we need to meet in arenas – but no matter how large a gathering, I'll still want us to have flowers and candles. I see groups of men and women meeting to discover their true selves and focusing the time and attention it takes to tune into the plan God has for each of our lives.

In my work, I've learned that many women hide their true selves because they fear judgment or rejection. They worry that who they are is too powerful or that what God wants for them is too splendid. I know men and women who have given up on being their authentic selves and who bury their potential under many defenses. Others have ignored the reality that God is there with a plan for them, and they give up on themselves just because other people have given up on them. When we decide to live out of our true selves we are seeing ourselves as God sees us.

Living Authentically and Reaching Higher

God loves who we have been, who we are, and who we can be. We just need to know very deeply that we are not our past, we are not our mistakes, and wherever we find ourselves on this particular day is exactly where we can begin to live more authentically. You can overcome anything, and you can get beyond simply surviving and move into a life where you thrive – if you are willing to work with God and be your true self. I believe this because I believe so strongly in the grace and forgiveness of God, and because I have witnessed this transformation in my own life and in the lives of many others.

I know we can accomplish great things when we work with God, because I see this principle at work in the lives of so many extraordinary people. Minister Mary Edwards is a powerful woman who saw the Divine within herself at a young age and knew she was much more than who others defined her to be. She faced the kind of life circumstances that could have limited her, but instead, she was inspired to reach higher.

"Are you pregnant, Mary?" asked my eighth-grade teacher.
"Yes." I confessed in a whisper. The full broomstick skirt I had made in my home economics class no longer concealed my protruding belly. At the tender age of thirteen, I was six months pregnant and had gotten that way on the day I lost my virginity. My teacher marched me to the principal's office.

It's been nearly fifty years since that difficult day, and I still remember my teacher and principal looking at me with a combination of sorrow and disgust. I also remember their piercing words. "What a tragedy. She was an honor roll student," my teacher said, putting my life in the past tense.

"And now all she will ever be is just another welfare statistic," the principal added.

Their words pierced my heart like arrows and echoed in my head for a long time. I was already overburdened with my own fears and insecurities, and adding their judgment and their pronouncement that I would be just another welfare statistic was hard to bear.

My mother took me to the doctor for an examination. A single parent herself, she struggled with five children and two jobs. She didn't need another mouth to feed. When the doctor suggested that because of my age I should have an abortion, my mother asked me what I wanted to do. What a dilemma! I was too young to be a mother, but the alternative seemed even worse to me. My childhood had been hard and I knew that motherhood would be even harder, but I made my choice. In spite of her deep and understandable disappointment, Mama said, "Well, then, we are going to have a baby!" She supported me and made the best of every circumstance. She was only thirty-one years old herself at that time and faced life with such courage!

My graduation day was only a few short weeks away, but I was not allowed to graduate with my class. As soon as they knew I was pregnant I was told to pack my things and leave. My mother picked me up from school and I walked away with a heavy heart and with my head down. My elementary school diploma, along with the honor roll designation and my achievement certificates were mailed to my home.

My life can be measured in a variety of statistics, but not the ones predicted by my teacher and principal. With the support of my mother and by the grace of God, I graduated from high school with honors at the age of 16, with a three year-old holding my hand. I have never been on welfare. I am an ordained minister. I was blessed to be married for twenty-one years to a wonderful man of God who was highly respected throughout the country. My husband and I received a Point of Light Award from former President George H. W. Bush for our community service work. In 2003, I was voted "One of the Most Influential African

American Women in Metropolitan Detroit." And when my husband passed in 2004, I established a ministry called Widows With Wisdom. In two short years, this ministry grew to include over sixty women, and requests for a similar outreach ministry have come to me from across the country and from Canada. In 2005, I published my fifth book and, over the years, I have served as a book coach for hundreds of writers helping them tell their stories. I have mentored many single mothers and young girls over these decades – emphasizing that they don't have to be "just another welfare statistic." And this year, I will celebrate my sixty-fourth birthday, and my son will turn fifty.

In my Widows with Wisdom ministry, we use Proverbs 24:6 as our foundational scripture and I find great comfort in the words: "In a multitude of counsel, there is safety." I found that safety, and I know it is there for every one of us.

I sense a healthy self-love in Mary's words, and know that each of us needs a strong sense of self in order to have the strength to be authentic and to be in-touch with our greatest potential. We need to love ourselves the way God loves us and to treat our body and soul with the highest regard. When we care for ourselves properly we become better decision makers. When we value and nurture ourselves, we become more careful about who we let into our space. When we walk with God we treat our body, mind, spirit, and our homes like the sacred spaces they are.

A Reflection of Your True Self

As I work with women and men from around the world, I see that the way people choose a relationship often reflects how they feel about themselves. This decision is such an important key to happiness that it is important to invite God into how we seek a relationship, and what we make of it once we call it into our lives. We benefit from seeking God's face as we choose our relationship and we can go significantly off-track if we are sloppy in this regard.

It is common that instead of waiting for the right person to come into our lives, we go ahead and choose based on who we know at the time. What a mistake to know full well that the person we are deciding to be with is not right one for us, or for God's plan for us, and stubbornly make the decision to proceed anyway.

We can give our love and our lives to someone simply because we are lonely and need a friend, rather than inviting God to help us find just the right person with whom to share our lives. Most times, this compromise of our deep integrity does not work, and the result is heartache for all parties. Making right and good choices in our life is a practice that takes a strong connection to God, and oftentimes a great deal of patience. But, once we have learned to make good choices, we are able to make better choices the next time. Mary Haskett writes about her experience inviting God into the process of finding the right husband, and how this led her to a relationship with a certain tall, distinguished man with silver-gray hair.

The sun was warm on my back. I sat on a bench in Springbank Park and made a heart-felt entry in my journal. *God, I want to ask you to help connect me to my husband, the one you have for me out in the world somewhere. Bless him today Lord, and direct his steps. I know you have the power to send him to this picnic table right now and that you could prompt him to talk to me. I feel ready for that to happen.*

I am a divorced mother. I had prayed that my marriage could be saved, but my prayers had not brought my husband back. Friends told me that God didn't allow remarriage, and that I must be content to stay alone for the rest of my life. But it had been thirty years, and surely the loving Jesus I've come to know didn't hold me responsible for my husband's actions and doesn't insist that I live alone when my authentic self knew that being with the right husband would fulfill me.

My friend Nancy, who was also alone, was the person who encouraged me to pray in this way. After reading a book by T.D. Jakes titled, *Woman Thou Art Loosed*, she became excited about overcoming the wounds of the past and moving on with her life, and her enthusiasm had rubbed off on me. We both felt strongly that God had good husbands somewhere out there for us, and so we decided to pray daily for these men we hadn't met yet and ask God to bless them.

The first day we prayed like this, Nancy saw, in her mind's eye, a tall, distinguished man with silver-gray hair who felt to her as if he was the husband for me. I joked with her about it sometimes. And as I stood singing in my church choir, I felt like shading my eyes from the bright lights and shouting "Are you out there?" But I had refrained myself.

After I wrote in my journal that morning, I made a trip to the hospital to visit my dear, gentle friend Fran, who was dying of cancer. I visited her every day until a very sad day when, back in the park with my journal, I wrote, *Fran's with You now Lord. I'll miss her so much and so will her husband and all of her friends and family. Comfort all of us Lord, and help us bless each other in whatever ways you see fit. Then, I continued writing about the other issue that was very much on my mind. How's my husband today, Lord? I pray all is well with him.*

As I drove from the park to the grocery store, I found myself thinking about Fran's husband and his request that I keep in touch. At the funeral, he had said he hoped we would continue to be friends and I had been out of touch for a while. Our connection came through Fran, and now that she was gone, I felt awkward and didn't know how to be a friend to him. I also knew that many people would visit and help him in his grief. I knew that although he would feel sorrow for a long time, he would be fine if he kept talking to people around him. As I checked the last item into the cart, I heard his name. Al. I dismissed it. At home, I put the groceries into the cupboard and then rushed off to choir prac- tice. I heard his name again. Al. "Lord, is this You speaking to me?" I said out loud. I was so busy. I had a zillion things to do. And I knew that Al had many friends and that they would keep in touch with him. I thought I could concentrate on other things. Al! I felt the voice insist again. "Okay, Lord, I promise I'll call him and see if I can be helpful."

I didn't know what to say when I called, but I tried to offer consolation. As we talked, I ended up telling him about my time writing in the park in the mornings. Perhaps if he wrote in a journal and talked to God, he would be comforted. We agreed I would pick him up and take him to the park the following morning. He was waiting for surgery on his hip, and wasn't driving much. This was a way for him to get some fresh air. In the park, he wanted to talk about Fran and their life together, and so I listened to him process his grief and together we read the condolence cards he had received. I had a lump in my throat. It was so hard to think about Fran not being with us all anymore.

In coming months, Al and I visited the park every so often. It was good for both of us to get out in nature. Before the cold weather set in, I suggested we have a picnic in the park. We sat under a tree and the lake was calm and the breeze was gentle. Now, he asked questions about me, my family, and how long I had been on my own. "I'm surprised no one has snatched you up," he said. "I admire you so much. I want you to know that Fran and I agreed that if God took one of us before the other, the one remaining should feel free to marry again." He choked up with tears. "I really care about you. Would you consider marrying me?"

I told him I would pray about it and we drove back to the city. My mind was racing and I felt a gamut of emotions. When I dropped him off, Al stood on the steps of his house waving good-bye and for a moment I froze looking at him and seeing him with new eyes. My hands tightened on the steering wheel and I swallowed hard. "Oh, my goodness, oh, my goodness," I said over and over again as I drove away. I had to phone Nancy and tell her that I was surprised to find a Godly man in my life – a tall, distinguished man with silver-gray hair!

Months later, it was spring again and Al and I were in the park. We sat close together and watched brilliant shafts of iridescent light radiate from the diamond engagement ring on my left hand. We smiled at each other with full hearts, understanding that God had arranged it this way.

Peace comes easily when we are in touch with God and act from our true self. This is when we can hear a still, small voice telling us everything will be alright. This voice also has the ability to help us self-correct by reminding us to get grounded when we become anxious or fearful. When we walk in our spiritual power, we are inviting God to help orchestrate our lives and we are not alone.

Our authentic self is our inner compass. It guides us and provides a powerful knowing that helps us trust the path of our lives and relax into letting our light shine. When we live in this light, we do not copy others, compare ourselves to others, criticize others, or engage our ego in unhealthy ways. When we are in touch with God and our true self, we are peace with who we are and our path to becoming more healthy and whole is made clear.

God wants us to live an abundant life full of heart and spirit. He also wants us to experience comfort, security, and safety. To arrive at this abundance, we need to stay in touch with our real self and remember that we are on God's timetable and that patience is an important virtue.

When you walk in your power, you will not be disappointed about how things are or ungrateful for the life you have. Instead, you will see that things are as they should be, and that everyday grace is all around you. I've talked to women who judge themselves harshly and who don't like the person they see in the mirror. I've talked to women who complain about the difficulty of their lives, and never feel like they have enough of anything. I remind them that many people who have everything money can buy are still deeply unhappy. The greatest happiness is always found within.

In the days when I had lost my money and was in despair, I still somehow managed to see myself as worthy of self-love and of God's love. I understood that I needed to get in touch with my authentic self and I didn't see myself as permanently broken or deeply unworthy. I accepted that things were difficult, but that there were things I could learn from the experience. Those thoughts, feelings, my prayers, and the time I spent reading the Bible sustained me. I know of many other men and women who have overcome much worse hurdles than I faced by holding fast to their true self and their faith in God. If you have this inner knowing, you cannot fall too far, you cannot fail forever. If you know who you are and stay connected to your true self, you can always come back to the center.

The Divine
: Chapter Eight

SENSING AND KNOWING THE DIVINE is one of the most important experiences each of us can have. It may not be possible to feel connected to God in every moment, but to have direct knowledge that we are not alone is something we can experience at the high points in our lives and even experience often in our average days if we pray, read the Bible, and go into silence and listen. We are not alone and nothing can separate us from the love of God. When you know how to get in touch with the Divine you'll want to return to that feeling as much as you can because it is an exquisite place to be.

I love Jamaica and spend as much time there as possible. A couple of years ago, I celebrated a memorable birthday at Sunset at the Palms, a small resort nestled in a lush tropical garden setting along a white sand beach and beautiful blue water. The tree-house-style guest room provided the feeling that I was safely nestled in the branches, and as I walked through the gardens, I reveled in the explosion of fragrant color of Canaan lilies, the sound of birds singing, and the wind moving gently through the trees. As I absorbed the beauty and grace of my surroundings, I knew the reason I loved this place so much was that, for me, it was just what God's presence feels like. I rested on the balcony in the trees on a beautiful white sofa, and it was so peaceful that I could totally surrender to the feeling of bliss. I thanked God for His creation and for the boundlessness of His love.

My life is made of many more challenging moments than those I spend soaking up the beauties of Jamaica, but seeking the Divine is the refuge I can try to find within myself every day. Of course, I want to connect with the Divine as much as I possibly can! Once any man or woman has a direct experience of the Divine, they feel a natural desire to spend as much time connected to God as possible.

Beauties of the Earth

God is the safe and beautiful place to which we can always return. We can work to cultivate this connection, seeking out the soul-nurturing experiences that fill us with grace. When we are full of grace, we have the inner resources to face the difficulties that are a part of life. With the experience of both the dark and light we learn that we can get through tough times, that relief can be found, and that no matter what happens, we are always assured of the love of God. Many of us find a direct experience of the Divine through nature. This connection with the natural world can offer incredible opportunities for healing and expansion. Lisa Cohen shares her experience of what she thinks of as the "coastal creator" in this story of her transformation.

Beads of sweat formed on my forehead and my heart raced. The city seemed to spin around me as I gasped for breath. With each step on the sidewalk, my dizziness increased. I prayed I could make it the final ten steps to my office building. I did not faint on the sidewalk in front of the hundreds of people on their morning commute, lattes in hand, and I'm grateful for this. My doctor was trying to help reduce the daily fear and panic that was wearing down my body and mind. A heart monitor and medication didn't control the panic attacks and my doctors were not able to identify the cause of my illness or address my symptoms effectively.

My desperation to feel better overwhelmed me. I painted after work to ease my internal frustrations. I drank smoothies and did yoga and any-thing else I knew to be good for my health. My attempts to take care of my spirit, soul, and body seemed to have failed. I felt swallowed-up by the world and was drowning in the chaos. I knew deep within myself, that a remedy must exist and that my life did not need to be this way.

A family vacation to the west coast of the United States provided a break from work and a chance to experience the evergreen trees and the fresh air. I had been to Oregon before, and remembered how it rejuvenated my spirit. This time, I hoped for some of that magic and per-haps even a cure for my ailments. I prayed to discover the *something* I so desperately needed.

We rented a small house on the Oregon coast, in a place called Cannon Beach. Grandparents, aunts, uncles and cousins joined my immediate family for a week. I was lucky, and had been able to travel to many amazing places all over the world, but none of them called to my soul the way Oregon did. Arriving after dark, I could smell the evergreens mixed with the salt from the Pacific Ocean. I opened the bedroom window and fell asleep to the sound of the crashing waves. The next morning, I quickly dressed and laced up my running shoes. My dad, uncle, and mom and I were going to run on the beach and I could not wait to get my feet on the sand.

I began slowly, allowing my body to warm-up, and then I focused my attention on the sight and sound of the crashing waves. The others ran ahead and I gave myself the gift of solitude and time for reflection. I was immersed in the vastness of nature and I felt gently held by my beautiful surroundings. As the shoreline curved, I lost sight of my family and experience the most magnificent connection to nature I had ever felt. My feet moved through the sand, I took in the crisp air and breathed deeply, and as I came around the next turn, I burst into tears at the sight of an immense volcanic rock that stood over two-hundred feet in the air and was partially submerged in the ocean.

It seemed to me that this enormous stone captured the power and essence of all that had been created. I stood alone with tears streaming down my face taking in nature's beauty and the tremendous power it holds. In my daily life, I had felt like an ant so often. I was surrounded by skyscrapers and honking horns and felt overwhelmed. Now, I was overwhelmed by the vastness of nature and my smallness in comparison, but what I felt was the unification of my soul with God.

I cried in response to the beauty of what I saw and also because I was experiencing a spiritual awakening. Something in me was coming to life. I had not been a religious person, but I craved the something that was missing in my life. On that morning, I found a sense of my own spirituality for the first time. This spirituality and connection was within myself and came through nature. God showed me my inner-strength and I felt the power to make changes in my life. I would allow myself to live my own way from now on. I would release the external pressure of feeling "I should" all the time. As soon as I realized that I could be connected to the Divine and be free I was deeply relieved, my body felt open to receiving new ideas and feelings, and I began the process of healing.

I returned from the trip to my life in the concrete of the city, but things were different inside me. I had taken a photo of Haystack Rock on Cannon Beach; I enlarged it and hung it in my bedroom. When I looked at the image, I remembered how my body felt on that beach and how my lungs opened in order to breathe deeply. A few months later, I had a major health scare and was told that perhaps I should put the next year of my life on hold and focus on my health. I decided I would live in Oregon. No longer would I feel trapped in the grind of a life that didn't suit me. I emptied my apartment and drove to the place where nature fueled my soul.

The trip with my family and the run on the beach had connected me to a belief in a greater power. I've heard Oregon's coast described as "God's country" and I would wholeheartedly agree. I have been able to make the most amazing and positive changes in my life, and now I am regularly in touch with the Divine. Over the past seven years, I have returned often to Cannon Beach, and during each visit I allow myself some space for reflection. Each time my feet touch the sand and I look out at Haystack Rock, I cry with a heart full of gratitude.

Circle of Love

It is a lovely truth that each of us responds to different places in unique ways. Some of us thrive in cities, while others seek in remote places. For some of us, family and friends hold the key to Divine connection, for others solitude is the touchstone to God. Can you remember the last time you sensed the Divine? What did it feel like, where were you, and what did it mean to you? Knowing how you can personally make a connection to God is the key to creating a life where you experience everyday grace and miracles.

Melissa Annette Santiago describes how she made a connection to the

Divine during an extraordinary time in her life, and how she was able to hold a powerful experience like a precious treasure that helped her for years to come.

The last time I saw my mother was the morning after she died. It was dawn – the time when the day's possibilities are formed, when the humid air condenses on the grass, and when the thick sea air pours itself out upon the parked cars on the streets and stray cats taking shelter. I was just waking from sleep, just becoming aware of my body, when I remembered that yesterday my mother had died suddenly and unexpectedly. I would not see her leave for work this morning or return home this evening. If I called her office to ask if I could go to my best friend's house after school, the only bit of her voice I would hear again was that of her message on the answering machine. Events of the day before flashed through my mind and felt unreal to me. I had seen my mother in the hospital, her body flattened against the hard metal of the coroner's cart, a plastic tube hanging from her mouth and pulling on her pink lips. These images replayed themselves again and again as I felt the loss of her. And then she appeared to me.

I could feel her presence around and within me, and felt her sending me strength and filling me with hope. Instead of seeing the morbid images of her dead body, I now felt her soul as being vibrant and very much alive. With my eyes still closed, I could see swirls of purples, greens, and blues. The colors seemed to contain her spirit and to dance in celebration at the discovery of a new home somewhere high above me. In this abundant color and surrounded by the love of God, I saw my mother's face – her gentle dark eyes, round cheeks, soft lips, and beautiful black hair. With my eyes still closed, I could see her leaning down to kiss my forehead. My warm tears slid down my temples dampening the pillow beneath my upturned face.

I did not turn or stir for fear that if I opened my eyes, I would be disconnected from the essence of her soul that hung above my bed and surrounded me. I wanted to hold onto this warmth and peace and the sense of knowing that she still existed and that she had come to comfort me. I understood that my mother wanted me to know the truth – that life does not end with our last breath. It is simply transformed to something greater. We are someone greater, and we go on to be with someone greater. My mother had been transformed into colors that danced and laughed and sang.

Later, as the vision faded, I heard the sound of whimpering and crying coming from down the hall. I opened the door of my parents' room and peered in to see my father holding my mother's purple and plaid nightgown over his face to silence his cries, and to take in the scent of her body still living in the cotton. I knew he was afraid of the time when her scent would fade and he would have no tie to her. I sat on the bed and cradled his head. I assured him that we would be fine, that she was not really dead. I knew, because I had experienced her presence, that she was not gone and that her love for us was boundless and would have no end.

Almost ten years later I still feel her with me. When I laugh, I hear her laughing. When I tease my husband, I hear her giggling with my father. During quiet moments with my sister, I imagine my mother and my aunt sharing their secrets. Life is repeating itself with the experiences and tenderness that pass through one generation to the next. God's love for each of us extends from one human being to another, awakening the soul of the thing it touches, and bringing a love of life through a newborn baby.

We are all connected through the love we receive, like links on a charm bracelet. Circular and timeless, love unites the past and the present. And now I understand that love does not disintegrate or fade. Love is like energy: it moves throughout time, taking with it the characteristics of those who came before, making the energy of love richer and deeper with every generation born into a loving home.

My mother extended God's devotion by loving her children unconditionally and selflessly. At the end of a twelve-hour day, when it would have been easier to prop my sister and me in front of the television, my mother instead chose to read us stories or play games with us. On the weekends, she served as our Girl Scout troop leader. Rather than sleep in on Sundays, she took us to church. My mother made difficult choices seem easy. I can easily imagine my mother as a new mom, holding me close to her in bed at night and looking into my eyes, trying to fill me with the truest nourishment my new soul needed – God's love. Her life's work was to love her husband and her children, and it is a job she continues to perform as an angel from Heaven.

Two days after my own daughter was born, as I was memorizing the tiny features of her face, I realized that I had not yet shared with her the three words I knew I must never forget to say to her each and every day. As I said, "I love you," I made the choice to mother my child in the same way I had been mothered. I looked into my daughters' warm brown eyes and told her I loved her, and her eyes focused for the first time. I thought that perhaps until that moment her soul had been waiting to have a reason to bloom. And now here she was, the result of generations of love that had begun with the Creator, and had moved through generations of ancestors, the *Tainos*, to my great-great grandparents, grandparents, and finally down to my own mother whose decision to love me had filled my life with meaning and joy.

Since that day, each time I hold my daughter and stare into the eyes that remind me so much of her father's and my own, I pray that my love for her will help her grow to be everything she is capable of being. I also give prayerful thanks for the love I've received all my life, including the love that came from my mother. A love that never ceases to soothe me, a love I know I will always feel.

What a gift it is to sense the presence of the Divine. It is an experience that transforms our life and one that we can hold as a precious treasure. At the times in my life when I have felt the presence of God most strongly, I have bowed my head to say a simple prayer, "Lord, I thank you for allowing me to sense your presence." His presence is a life-changing thing to experience and when we share the stories of how we have been attended to by God we support others in being open to experience the Divine.

Finding Answers

There are times when we move forward knowing we are on track and are supported by God, but when we experience what I think of as life's little hiccups, we can also turn to God for answers to our large and small questions about how to live. It is tempting to be consumed with worry or to project our present situation into the future and loose faith, but if we draw close to God we can sense his presence and receive his guidance. Suzanne Windon faced a difficult decision as she stood at an important crossroads in her life. I find it charming that coffee became her symbol when she asked for confirmation and assistance from the Divine.

I breathe deeply, savoring the aroma of the coffee. Gavin brings me a cappuccino. I sink back into the couch, shoulders relaxed, my guard finally down. The music is loud, too loud for my taste, with a strong beat that reverberates through the table. The noise competes with the loud sound of the coffee grinder churning the beans I've just purchased and will soon take home. Paintings of Mayan Indians decorate the walls of this coffee shop, along with framed posters advertising movies in English. The lighting is soft and a football game is playing on the large television screen over the counter.

In this stimulating cacophony, I enjoy a sense of connection to the other westerners who congregate here. In a city of three million people, very few of whom are westerners, the coffee shop is one of the few places where I don't stand out and where I can enjoy a feeling of anonymity.

I slouch back onto a couch near a tinted window and watch the procession of men, women, children, and dogs who pass by on foot, on bicycles, and in cars. The road seems to be permanently under construction – like many roads here – half dug up with throngs of people intently dodging potholes.

On the other side of the street, a man cooks noodles in a large outdoor wok. No doubt he works for the restaurant whose painted windows declare one of their specials – handmade dumplings. The noodles look good. The dumpling restaurant is on the bottom floor of a high rise building and from my vantage point, I can see the top of what will be a brand new building down the street. Seven men precariously balance on a framework of steel high in the sky, a yellow crane swings back and forth above them.

I sip my cappuccino. Escaping to the comforting familiarity of a western café is pretty expensive, but it is also a source of great pleasure for an Australian woman working in China. Life in China and coffee are an unusual mix. I sip slowly, drowning in self-pity. It had seemed so right to move to China. God's direction had seemed so clear and so obvious to me at one point in time. But today, I consider leaving in defeat. Who was I fooling? The truth is I am stumbling along in a language and culture not my own and things aren't going well. The chaos of this densely populated city is wearing me out and I want to go home. Something different has to happen if I'm going to stay. I raise my coffee mug to heaven and take a vow. "Until you reconfirm my call to China, Almighty God, not another drop of coffee will pass my lips." Desperate times call for desperate measures.

The following morning, I sip my cup of tea. "Please, Lord, if you want me here, reconfirm my call." In the office an hour later, I discover an e-mail message from a woman I've never met. She writes; *You don't know me, but I was in the congregation on the evening your church commissioned you to go to China. God gave me a vision that night but I didn't share it with you. Yesterday, I was sitting in a meeting at work when suddenly, out of the blue, I was hit with the impression that I must write to you and tell you about that vision. I felt I couldn't rest until I'd done it, so I got your email address from the church. In the vision, you were standing in a bright light. Beside you was an opening in the ground. There were people trapped there and it was dark and frightening in the ground. You worked very hard and finally pulled one person out into the light. That person stood by you and put his arm out with yours into the ground again, and together you pulled another person out, and then another. Eventually, a big crowd stood in the light, working together.*

I just want you to know that God has equipped you and sent you to China at this point in time for a purpose. Be encouraged.
I have planned to meet a friend for prayer later in the day, but now I quickly pull out my cell phone and sent a text message through my

grateful tears, *Meet @ coffee shop @ 12, OK?*

A few months have passed. I sit at the coffee shop with a paper bag of freshly ground coffee beans in front of me, a cappuccino in my hand. I gaze out at the bustling community in which I happily live and productively work. I raise my cup to heaven. "One day at a time. And I'm not doing it alone. Thank you, Father."

This request for confirmation had two important parts. First, Suzanne had to be willing to seek Divine guidance and bring an open heart to her question of what to do next. The second, and equally important part, was that the woman who felt that it was imperative to be in touch with Suzanne to share her story of the vision, had to act on that powerful prompting with faith and clarity. Both women were in touch with the Divine and both acted their part in ways that allowed them to be of service to God. I am reminded of the story of Queen Esther in the scriptures. At a critical point, she called her people together to pray and fast, and then she surrendered to the king knowing that God's will would be done. She surrendered to the Holy Spirit saying that if she perished she could accept that, but she was going to listen and be guided by the Holy Spirit. Her surrender was a gift to God and all was well.

When we move from where we are to where our Creator desires us to be, we see, feel, think, and even act differently. We can experience much more in life if we move beyond our own ideas and the actions we alone can take, and instead invite the Divine to provide vision and momentum in our lives.

Barbara Williams is someone who wants to walk with the Divine. She doesn't like to get stuck in her comfort zone and so she looks carefully at things that happen in her life in order to see God. What she expected to be a simple fishing trip turned out to be a lasting lesson for her.

My husband asked me to go fishing with him and I accepted his invitation without inquiring about it. I assumed he just wanted me to be there with him. Once we arrived at the fishing spot, he prepared three poles for casting. There were two of us and three poles, but I wasn't paying attention to the details of *his* trip because I had my own plans.

My husband carefully caught bait by net fishing first for the smaller fish with which he would catch the larger fish he was really after. He baited the hooks of the first pole and looked over at me, asking if I was okay where I was. I said that I was just fine. He had brought a comfortable chair for me to sit in, and I had brought along two very interesting books and I was diving into them.

He carefully placed the first fishing pole in the ground near the water in front of me as he baited the second pole. Then he looked over at me with a puzzled look on his face and called out, "Are you okay over there?" I again said, "Oh yes, I'm fine!" He looked at the pole in front of me and back to where I was sitting in my chair so far behind it. He looked at the second pole and then at the third pole he was ready to bait and said, "Honey, you won't be able to hold the pole in the water over there where you are." We both got the point. You see, he and I had different plans for this fishing trip. He had three poles, planning that I would use one of them and that together we would catch many fish. He had brought me a chair to relax in, but thought I would relax as I fished. I had brought two books and had no intention whatsoever to actually fish.

Once we were on the same page and had three poles in the water, it was supper time! We worked well together and constantly pulled in one of the poles with a fish on the line. It turned out we needed each others' help to get things done. As I reeled the lines in with fish, he would add more bait to the lines and cast them back.

I loved helping my husband that day and I have often thought about that fishing experience and what it has in common with our relationship with our Creator. We can be His hands to work, feet to move, eyes to see, mouth to speak, and His ears to hear. Whatever and however He needs us, we can put down our own plans to help fulfill His. The result will be abundant blessings. His plans may need us to move from our cool and comfortable spot and require us to do some work, but we will be able to accomplish His will and enjoy the results.

I accept that the Joy of the Lord is truly my strength. I accept the many blessings God has in store for my Life. I believe God always will work things out for my highest good. I believe our job is to get our thoughts and actions right so that we can produce the right results. Our comfort comes from knowing that no matter where we are, God is and will always be there to guide us and show us the way.

Becoming a
Change Agent

WE EACH HAVE DIVINE POTENTIAL WITHIN US, and that is why we can change our lives for the better and be an agent for change in the world. Our divine seed is like an acorn that may seem small to us at times, but it holds the potential to become a great oak tree. As an agent of change, we can allow God's light to shine through us and we can rise above the limits of our own ego by setting aside what I call the three C's. I think we need to stop *copying, comparing,* and *criticizing,* since these are such limiting behaviors. What we need to focus on instead is our commitment to making a difference and our ability to be an agent for change.

I don't believe anyone needs to die of hunger in this world, and that if good people everywhere decided hunger was no longer acceptable, we would find a way to end it. It seems to me that evil continues to exist in our world because good people make the decision to do nothing. Each of us has a responsibility to make a difference in the world, but that doesn't mean we have to shoulder the entire burden and lose our lives in the process. I think too often people feel that if they can't do everything, they have an excuse to opt to do nothing. The proper balance is found in the middle ground. We can consistently lend a hand and take care of our own lives properly at the same time. We just need to consciously make a difference on an ongoing basis, knowing that it will add up over our lifetime.

We can all respond to a sense of calling about how to act for God as an agent for change. As my friend S. Brenton Rolle found, it may be just a matter of acting with integrity in the moment and listening to the Divine within us when we receive the call.

It was late in the evening on the night of my fathers' wake in Delray Beach, Florida. I was sitting in the church surrounded by family and friends and I was full of emotion. I was still receiving phone calls from my family since many of them were coming in from out of town and needed directions to the church. My phone kept vibrating and I kept getting up and stepping outside. This new call came in as an unavailable number. I walked outside the church assuming it would be a relative. I answered only to hear a stranger's voice ask, "Can you talk to me?"

I was caught off guard so I said, "I'm sorry what did you say?"

Again the voice asked, "Can you please talk to me?" I was puzzled, but it felt right to say yes. The woman was obviously distraught. I spoke softly and asked her how I could help her and what she wanted to talk about. I wanted to temporarily escape my grief and to try and comfort her if I could. She explained that her husband had moved them from their home in Canada to the United States, and that she didn't know anyone she could turn to. I had no training in crisis counseling, but I knew I did not want to hang up or turn her away, even though this was a stressful time for me as well. I understood that I could do some good if I listened to her and let her know God's love was accessible. She said her husband had left her. I asked if he had left the room, the house, or if they were divorced. She explained that they had just had a big fight and that he had left the house. "Are you hurt?" I asked.

"No, nothing like that. He didn't hit me, he's just very abusive and yells and screams at me."

"Do you have any family or friends who can come and see about you?"

"No, he moved me away from my family and friends. I don't even know what number I dialed just now. I picked up the phone and called whoever I could reach."

"Oh, I see. What's your name?"

"Alexis."

"Hello, Alexis, since you told me your first name I'll tell you mine. I'm Brent."

We were total strangers who were both in an extreme situation and the feeling of the conversation was intense and surreal. "Alexis, are you of a particular faith? Are you Christian, are you Muslim or Jewish?" "I'm Catholic."

"Do you have a priest you can talk to?" At this point I wondered if she was suicidal. She was obviously alone wherever she was. She could have been safely at her house or on top of a bridge for all I knew. "Alexis, I'm a Christian too and I want you to say a prayer with me." I didn't know what prayer I was going to say but I knew that when I feel upset and off-center I feel comforted by saying the Our Father. "Alexis, I want you to say the Our Father with me, and afterward I'll tell you why."

"Tell me now."

"You are calling me on the night of my father's wake. I am standing outside the church. He died on Christmas morning."

"Oh my God, I'm so sorry."

But before she could complete her apology I said, "No, I'm not telling you this to make you feel bad about calling, I'm saying it because even though this is going on, I want you to know that it was no accident that you reached me. I will stand out here and talk to you as long as you need me to, because that's what my father would have wanted me to do."

I could feel my voice trembling as I realized that at least some portion of the kindness and graciousness that was in my father's heart and spirit was in me.

"No, I want you to go back to your father's wake."

"Alexis, tell me you are not going to hurt yourself."

"I won't."

"I needed to hear you say it. I told you my name and I'll also give you the number you dialed, so that if you need to call someone again you can call me."

"I'm not going to hurt myself."

"Are you sure?"

"Yes, I'm sure."

There was a long silence and then she said, "Thank you."

We continued to talk for a few more minutes and when I hung up I saw that the funeral director had come outside to check on me. I told him what had happened. He said, "Man, after what you've been dealing with, I can't believe you took the time to talk to that lady."

I don't know what happened to Alexis and I may never know. What I do know is that I managed to speak to her from my heart as I tried to convey God's love to her. I wanted her to know that a stranger cared. Looking back on this experience, I think God was showing me something about myself. I learned that compassion can make the experience of life richer and that we can offer each other God's love at any time and place.

Little things do make a big difference in the world, and Brent's response is a wonderful reminder that through a simple act of everyday grace we can serve the Divine. When we act from the heart we act for God.

I enjoy the lively spirit in which Christine Miles approaches the challenge of being an agent of change in a story she shares with us about her humble sausage rolls.

Our church announced a special fundraising project. Each person who registered would be given ten dollars with the challenge to make it grow into a larger donation. I felt the right thing for me would be to make sausage rolls and sell them. I could make delicious home-made, whole meal, flakey pastry using low-fat butter and a tasty filling. I knew they would be a hit. I was so busy with three part-time jobs, raising three children with my husband, being involved in children's ministries at church, and teaching religious education at school, that I didn't see how sausage rolls could fit into my schedule.

God and I chat regularly, and this time He came to me. Our conversation went like this:

God: Christine, make sausage rolls. Please.

Me: Now, God? Where will I possibly fit that into my day?

God: I will provide time. Make sausage rolls. Glorify my name.

Me: But, God. I'll be inundated with orders. I won't be able to keep up.

God: I am in control. Make sausage rolls.

God knows by now that our silly conversations won't go on forever. He knows I have learned to bow to His will. But He also knows that I have to state my case before I agree to things. I know that I have to challenge myself to be an agent of change, but I also know I can challenge God too.

Me: Okay, God. I'll make the sausage rolls. But I need you to provide me with the energy and the right number of orders. Remember, I hate to get behind and feel stressed, so please only send the number of orders I can fulfill.

I told five people about the fundraiser and my sausage rolls. The word spread rapidly. The first day, I sold twenty-four dozen sausage rolls. I was blessed during my sausage-roll-making-time because it became an opportunity for meditation, prayer, and singing songs of praise to God. My heart was light as I kneaded the pastry, made the filling, and formed the rolls. Sometimes I got up early. Sometimes I stayed up late. God was good. God cared for me. There was one week when we had friends come to stay. As is my habit, I talked to God. "God, I've got people staying next week. I think I need a little break. If it's in Your plan." That week I only had orders for ten dozen sausage rolls. I praised God.

I took sausage rolls to neighbors who lived alone and this provided an opportunity to share God with them. I gave sausage rolls to a friend who had an ailing mother. She asked to come to church with me and returned home delighted with our church facility and program. "Glorify My name," He said, and I did.

There is a theory that the way to a man's heart is through his stomach. God knows this. As my agnostic husband ate my sausage rolls, he said. "You must really believe in your church to do this." Glorify My name!

Each week for the next ten weeks, I supplied between twenty-four and thirty dozen sausage rolls. By the end of ten weeks I couldn't stand the sight of butter, pastry, or sausage rolls. But by the end of ten weeks, my ten-dollar note had multiplied fifty-eight times and the conversation with my husband had continued. Derek said, "I've decided I'll come to church with you once a month." Oh, God. You have been revealed to those who didn't know You, through a humble sausage roll.

Not only can we be agent of change for others, we can also take care of ourselves and make sure we commit to positive change in our own lives. Ask for change, surrender to change, and change will come with God's help guiding you at every step.

Re-entry
: Chapter Ten

EACH OF US HAS THE NEED TO CENTER and come back to our most authentic self. I think of this process as re-entry. After a big change or a crisis, it is essential to come back to the center, but it is also equally important to attend to the need to re-enter as a daily maintenance habit.

I understood the need for re-entry only after I had lost nearly everything and was beginning to pull myself together and recover. When I realized that I wasn't going to wither up and die, I began to take care of myself again. When I understood it was better to open the mail and answer the phone rather than avoid the bills and other problems, I started to see that to do things differently I needed to be at my best. It was then I began to devise ways of getting back, not to my "old self," but to a "better, newer self." In this process, I discovered that I needed special care to stay grounded. I figured out that if I treated myself to a movie, a long walk, or an inexpensive dinner out I could love myself back into balance. I learned that to recover from the stresses of every day I needed to walk to a place I loved and just sit and breathe. This self-care helped me become stronger at my core; it helped me know that I could cope with anything.

I practice re-entry every night before I go to sleep. I give myself a transition out of the world and into my connection with myself and with God. I set aside some time during which I do not expose myself to any negativity. I don't watch the news just before I go to bed. Instead, I read something motivational or listen to relaxing music, and my last thought before going to sleep is to say a prayer. In the morning, I also begin my day with prayer as a way to re-establish my connection to myself and God. Then, I make myself a cup of coffee and sit out on my balcony, watching the boats in the marina and planning how I will have a productive and joy-filled day. These things take only a few minutes but they ground the rest of the day in what is most important.

As I was moving out of a very difficult time a few years ago, I found that I could do at least one thing every day that would give me confidence. At that time, my confidence was so eroded that I was very vulnerable in this area. As I worked to change my life, I began my day with affirmative statements about why I was striking out in new directions, and I turned my goals into affirmative statements with which to begin the day. I would say aloud, "I am re-entering my life and I am building an even better future."

Learning the skills of re-entry will fill your soul and connect you to God. I invite you to think about where you are experiencing vulnerability in your life right now, and make sure that at the beginning of your day you take a few minutes to "re-enter" with a prayer and with affirmations that address that particular issue. This self care will help you create the joy and abundance you seek and will support you in living the life you are meant to live.

Divine Abundance

Suzanne Windon shares a story about her celebration of abundance that illustrates how we can fully appreciate and give thanks for the sense of plenty that can be part of every day. Caring for what we have with respect is one way we can show our gratitude. At the heart of her story is the idea that God wants us to use and appreciate what we are given, and pass it on generously as well.

The ming-blue, jazzed-up sporty little Hyundai seemed to have my name on it. The desire I expressed for a sporty type of car had been a joke really. I'd never even prayed specifically for it. A car of some kind, yes. But not one like this! Returning from eight years in China with only $1,470 Australian in savings, I was a bit stumped. I knew I needed a car of my own if I was to get a job and have a nice normal life during this time of sabbatical. However, $1,470 doesn't go far when you're talking about a car.

As I casually looked around, it became a running joke with my friends that all the cars I admired were metallic blue or green sports vehicles. "There's a car for Suzanne," someone would say as a snazzy little thing whizzed by. I had expensive taste, it seemed. Unfortunately, I also only had AU $1,470.

"I wouldn't really want a sports car," I demurred a number of times to whomever would listen. "I'd be scared of its power. I just want a normal little car that looks a bit like a sports car."

I had the loan of a clunky big car for six weeks as I settled back into Australia and reported back to churches and supporters. About four weeks into that time, I was no closer to purchasing a car. My cell phone rang. Some old family friends were on the line. "God told us to buy a car for you. A friend is selling a car right now and we feel strongly that we should buy it for you."

They explained there were only three catches to this gift. First, my friends lived about 125 miles from my home, but needed me to come see the car right away. Second, the car needed to be registered and insured by me. Third, it would take two more weeks for the car to be ready – it had been in an accident months earlier and needed to be repaired. My friends would pay for the repairs as part of the purchase price and then give me the car.

Amazingly, the city they lived in was exactly where I happened to be when I received the phone call. "I'll pop over right now, shall I? I'm just a few miles away!" I was a little worried about registering and insuring the car. What was I getting myself into, and could I afford even this part of the deal? Beggars can't be choosers, but I wasn't exactly a beggar, or was I?

When I laid eyes on that little car, I knew I was no beggar. Indeed, I felt as if I was the daughter of a king. Of course, we all are daughters and sons of a king and He provides beyond all expectation. My car was ming-blue, a sporty metallic blue-green, with a spoiler, mag wheels and a huge decal down each side. It was my dream come true. Under the hood, it was just another little putt-putt car, but to me it was spectacular.

To register the car wasn't inexpensive, and before insuring it, I was re-quired by the insurance agency to fit the car with an immobilizer. All totaled, the bill came to $1,480. It just so happened that a man had given me $10 at church that Sunday, for "whatever." God had provided exactly, yet again.

Two weeks later, I had to return the borrowed clunky car, which also happened to be exactly the day when I could pick up "my" car. I handed over the keys and hopped on a train north. My friends met me at the train station in that sporty and absolutely beautiful ming-blue car!

The first stop was the motor registry office. They issued me a license plate that read YRG 790. I thought that surely the letters stand for, "You aRre Great." The car is great, but even greater is the One who had provided exactly what I had dreamed about but never really hoped for. Every day, that car and I traveled the fifty mile round-trip to what turned out to be my dream job – another special surprise from God. The job just happened to finish right before I was scheduled to return to China.

Two years down the track, I handed that sporty car back to my benefactors, just one day before their own car developed major mechanical problems. God's timing was impeccable. A few private tears were shed as I parted with the car that was for me such a tangible expression of God's love and care, and then I stepped onto the plane. YRG 790, truly You aRe Great, God! Thank you.

Soul-nourishing Pleasures

I'm sure that taking appropriate delight in the things we have and in the soul-nourishing pleasure of our days makes our Creator happy. As I plan my week, I make sure that every day includes at least one act of re-entry. The things that make me feel grounded tend to include going for a walk while concentrating on feeling powerful and whole, going to church, attending to a particular detail of my business with special care, calling a friend to find out how she is doing and reassuring her that I am well, treating myself to a trip to a museum or to the movies, enjoying breakfast at a nice hotel, or relaxing with a cup of coffee and a newspaper while sitting near the water.

I understand that parents may say, "Your re-entry idea sounds great, but with our family duties we just don't have the time for this sort of thing." I encourage parents to teach re-entry skills to their children, and to take on this challenge of self-care as a family. The ability to ground ourselves is such a key part of living a fulfilling life that it seems reasonable that we would learn and practice these skills together. Many of us have had to learn about the need for self-care the hard way. Imagine how wonderful it would be to grow up knowing how to maintain your connection to God and to your most authentic self because of the example and encouragement of your parents. What a gift you can give your children when you pass along this practice.

Do you know what helps you re-enter your life feeling refreshed and grounded? What can you do to add at least one re-entry activity to every day of the week? I recommend that you note your re-entry ideas and track them in your journal or schedule. Treat yourself to the small things that help you feel supported. I've found a great place to get an inexpensive manicure and pedicure every once in a while, and I've also found ways to take advantage of standing room tickets to Broadway shows. I always look for opportunities to enjoy free events and I try to pay attention to how I can expand my list of re-entry activities.

As I was coming back into my life after a difficult time, I noticed a radical shift. When I attended to self-care and soul care I felt more grounded and powerful and I noticed that people around me sensed my joy and my confidence and wanted to spend time with me. It took a while for me to stop being afraid of not having enough money, and it took time before I could relax and trust again. But my affirmation was that I would get my joy back, and I did. Now, I work to maintain my joy every day. I hope you will join me in practicing the re-entry rituals that suit you and that provide you with a sense of Divine abundance. Explore the pleasures of your life and know that this will connect you to your authentic self and to God.

Surrendering to Grace

WE HAVE ALL HEARD HOW IMPORTANT IT IS TO SURRENDER to God, but for many of us actually doing so is quite a challenge. Surrender means to let go and turn things over to a greater power and that can be difficult if we don't have the faith to trust in God and give in to grace. I talk to many men and women who have the desire to let go and let God, but who just don't now how.

For me, surrendering to grace means doing my best and then waiting for an answer from God. In the past, I have waited on God many times and felt I was not getting an answer that I could recognize. Through long experience, I have learned that the answer might not be immediate and that it may come in a form I don't expect. These experiences have taught me the difference between playing at surrendering – while keeping an eye on God and without exercising true faith – and *really* surrendering, which involves honestly giving it up to God and trusting that He will work things out in ways that are for my highest good.

God Will Provide

Many times we only see the hand of God and the wisdom in how things unfold years after a particular event in our lives. Of course, there are also those wonderful and simple experiences of grace that show us that God can also provide in direct and obvious ways. Lora Woodhall found herself in a bind and invited God into the situation, asking for direct assistance and finding everyday grace as a result.

> "Lord," I prayed, "I don't know how to input my data into SPSS, and I don't understand the statistical terms and tests. You know everything. You designed the universe. Please help me understand how to do this."

As I gazed out at the beauty of the ocean, I felt enormously frustrated. Nothing I tried had worked; I just couldn't make sense of this statistical program. At home in Toronto, it had looked easy. But now, I was living on a tiny island with four other people and running a marine research station. I had no internet access and only intermittent phone service. A generator provided electricity, but supplies were brought in by boat from Exuma, a larger island with a population of about four thousand, a thirty minute boat ride away. Along with my duties as island manager, I was writing my final research paper to complete my degree. I had four weeks to finish the paper, and, without being able to use the computer program, I couldn't analyze my data. There was no one to turn to but God.

A few days later, I went to greet a marine scientist who was joining us to conduct research. Although she was initially scheduled to come alone, she was accompanied by her husband. As we walked to their quarters together he explained that he had made a last-minute decision to come along on the trip and commented that he had obviously made the right choice. Smiling at the evident pleasure he was taking in the beauty of our surroundings, I asked about his work. "I'm a professor," he replied. I explained that I had taught high school science at one point and asked what he taught. "Statistics." Stunned, I blurted, "What area of statistics?

Somewhat puzzled that I would be so interested, he replied, "I teach a statistical program called SPSS; Statistical Package for the Social Sciences. Have you heard of it?"

I looked at him in astonishment. "Really? I'm writing a research paper under a tight deadline and have been having difficulty with that program. Would you be willing to help me with it?"

Smiling, he said "Sure, I'd be very happy to help. How about tomorrow morning?" I returned to my office and praised God. This was incredible! He was there bright and early the next morning, ready to teach me. He listened attentively as I explained that I was investigating whether boys and girls learn science differently. After I showed him my surveys and observations, he made several suggestions about how I could analyze my data. Then for the next hour, he helped prepare the program for my particular data sets, showed me what tests to run, and explained statistical terms. At the end of our session, all I had to do was input my data, interpret the program's output, and finish writing my paper. I thanked him profusely and he said that it was his pleasure.

My heart overflowed with gratitude to my awesome God. He'd heard my prayer and connected me to a professor of statistics, one who just happened to specialize in the very program I needed to understand. And this professor loved his time on the island and genuinely enjoyed being of assistance to me. Truly, God is good!

Lora Woodhall surrendered to God in a lovely way and in this case, it seems to have been relatively easy for her. But having faith in God's grace can be a very difficult thing to do. It's important to remember that surrendering to God is not weakness. In fact, true surrender requires great strength and courage. It can be very challenging to give up our need to control. Exhibiting truth faith can be one of the hardest things we do.

Putting God First

I struggled to learn lessons about surrendering to Grace after I closed my law office. I had felt that God was calling me to be a speaker and I was excited as I began to offer my services. As a lawyer, I had seen contracts for major speakers, and so I followed that model. I knew I wasn't at that stage in my career so I offered my services at less than major speakers' rates, but I was still asking too much because I was just starting out. It isn't surprising to me in retrospect that I wasn't immediately successful, but at the time it was devastating. Two years into the work, I was barely making it, and yet I knew I felt led to do this work, so I was confused. I cried out to God, "Please tell me if I am doing the right thing." The answer I received was, "Surrender. Let go."

As I tried to understand these words, I finally saw clearly that I had been working from the level of ego. I had wanted the money and recognition of success, but I wasn't as tuned-in as I needed to be about how my work could really serve others. I needed to shift my emphasis on working to achieve personal success and instead surrender to something and someone much greater than me. That's when I understood that I had been failing because I had not yet surrendered to the plan God had for me. I had to "let go" of my past and my past failings, I had to let go of past hurt and I had to really learn how to trust God.

One of the past dramas that was limiting me in the new life I was trying to create was my attitude about money. I was always taking one step forward and ten steps back. I made money and lost money in ways that didn't serve my higher purpose because I didn't yet have real respect for money. This problem was evident in things like getting four parking tickets, then neglecting to pay the fines, even when they were relatively small. When I finally faced my responsibility to pay, I owed almost a thousand dollars. That was certainly not being a good steward of my resources. I also had a pattern of hiring someone to do work and then ending up doing the work myself. I didn't accept the responsibility for making a bad decision and I didn't work to solve it proactively. My failures forced me to look at my behavior, and when I decided to surrender my money to God, things finally shifted. I started to think of my resources as God's money and I prayed to be a good steward of that money.

I understood right away that I would have to give God His share and that one tenth of everything I earned needed to flow directly back to Him. I started rushing to place God's money in the offering plate as my first financial priority. Once I did this, I felt happy and felt safe. It was an act of surrender that really counted and I could feel the difference.

Surrendering to grace has many manifestations. For me, it has always had to do with my experience of prosperity. Once I finally said, "God, what I have is Yours," a big shift happened in my life. I no longer cared about chasing recognition or money. I simply worked with an open heart and the money I needed arrived. I had been chasing money and once I stopped chasing it, it started to find me. I almost could not believe it. As I stepped out of my own way, my income expectations were exceeded and, of course, the first thing I did was to pay tithes.

An Invitation

There is something pure about the right action it takes to surrender. Eve Eschner Hogan experienced a gentle lesson in letting go and letting God when she felt inspired to create a beautiful and peaceful environment and invited God to be a part of it.

About a year ago, my husband and I moved to a beautiful Maui property complete with a stream, fruit trees, tropical flowers of many kinds, and a huge, ten-thousand square-foot greenhouse. The greenhouse posed a bit of a problem for us since we didn't know what to do with it. At first, we thought it a detriment to the property and even considered tearing it down, but as time went by, God began "planting seeds" about what might grow there.

A vision of a peace garden began to unfold and I named the property, The Sacred Garden of Maliko. I followed this spiritual impulse and began building a labyrinth under a beautiful grove of Kukui trees. I had in mind creating something like the Chartres Cathedral labyrinth as a walking meditation and I envisioned a sacred space where people could come and experience the beauty and tranquility of the garden.

One day, while my sister was visiting, we drove to the other side of the island to escape the long rainy spell we were having on our side. As we drove, an idea came to me and I said, "You know what we need? We need a giant Buddha for the greenhouse. I want one that has a really sweet, peaceful presence that people will feel the minute they walk in."

My sister thought it was a lovely idea, but then I proceeded to explain why the idea was pretty much impossible. I had no idea where to get a giant Buddha on a small island, and if I gave money to an importer to get me one, he may not pick one out that had the quality and presence I was looking for – after all, not all Buddha statues are created equal. If I went to Bali or somewhere else to get the right Buddha, I would have to pay for shipping and figure out how to get it back. I had no idea how or where to get one. I just knew that the sacred garden needed one and that I had few resources. This conversation went on a few more minutes with no apparent solution, and then I looked over toward what we had hoped would be the sunny side of the island.

Unfortunately, it was still raining on that side too, so while we waited for the rain to clear, we stopped at the bamboo store to see if they had any trim we could use to decorate the greenhouse. When we pulled up to the store, we found it was closed. I felt defeated, but then I noticed that the used furniture store next door was just opening. "Well, let's go look at furniture while we wait for the weather to clear."

We had taken a few steps inside when I exclaimed, "There he is!" Just inside the front door of the furniture store was the most beautiful, and the sweetest giant Buddha I had ever seen. I stood in awe, my mouth and my heart open. He was carved from solid wood and was five feet tall, four feet wide, and weighted around six-hundred pounds. The sales lady offered her assistance and sat behind her desk to let us look around. I studied the Buddha, checked his price tag, and then walked to her desk and sat down. "Here is the problem. I love that Buddha, but I can't afford that Buddha." "Well, make an offer!" She said cheerfully. I had no idea where to begin "making an offer" because I was still trying to grasp the reality that we had actually found the right giant Buddha for the peace garden without even officially Buddha shopping!

Seeing that I was speechless, my sister jumped in and made an offer that was not quite half of what they were asking. The saleslady said, "Let me check with the owner of the shop and see what he says." Then, in true sales-person fashion she added, "If he says yes, are you prepared to buy the Buddha today?" My sister and I assured her that we were prepared to take the giant Buddha home today. "Give me a minute." And she picked up the phone while my sister and I made our way back to the Buddha.

I whispered to the smiling Buddha, "If you want to come home with me to be a blessed part of the sacred garden, you are going to have to make this work because I just can't spend more than this."

Very quickly, the saleswoman walked over and said, "You are never going to believe this. A man has been negotiating for this Buddha all week long, going back and forth with the owner of the store and the consignees – the owners of the Buddha. They finally agreed on the rock bottom price they would accept from him yesterday, and the buyer was supposed to come in and pay for it by five o'clock last night, but he never showed up. You two walked in the moment we opened this morning and offered that exact amount. The owner of the store didn't even have to ask the consignees, because he already knew they'd take this price. The Buddha is yours."

My heart leapt. I couldn't believe it. As I paid for the Buddha, my mind tried to race to catch up with the fact that only about fifteen minutes had passed from the inspiration of the idea to finding and purchasing the statue. The sacred garden continues to unfold gently, as God reveals each new piece of the puzzle to me – while I sit peacefully in front of a sweet, smiling Buddha.

Turning Ourselves Over

When we surrender to serving God we see the everyday grace that surrounds us. We need only ask for answers, listen quietly, and surrender to what we feel God is asking of us. Karen Elengikal faced a harrowing situation where her life hung in the balance, but she was comforted when she turned her life over to God.

If ever there was a defining moment in my life, it was the evening of June 30, 2003. As I was rushed to the hospital in an ambulance, I put my life into God's hands. My prayer was, "Lord, either take me safely into Your presence, or please, allow me to completely recover." Within minutes of arriving at the hospital, it was confirmed that I was having a heart attack. Injections were given to unblock my arteries, but still the pain continued. Another injection was administered, but to no avail. I remember the moment I drifted into unconsciousness, and then, some time later, I remember waking to the sound of someone calling my name.

My heart had stopped twice, and I had been given five electric shocks, and heart massage. It really was a miracle that I was still alive. An angiogram showed that I had experienced a rare heart attack – a dissected coronary artery. The main right artery had split from top to bottom.

I knew why I had survived. The nurses who attended to me during the emergency told me they felt the presence of God in the room throughout the crisis. I understood there was more for me to do in this life and that the Lord was preserving me for this work, despite the incredible odds. I was only forty-one and the mother of five sons under the age of ten. The event was very traumatic for us all.

Six months later, in January 2004, a bigger test of faith was presented to me when our local family doctor confirmed that I was pregnant. This news sent shock waves through my soul. My husband and I had been told while I recovered from the heart attack that I must not become pregnant. Most women have heart attacks only after child-bearing age. But because I was still in the age range where I could have another child, this was a huge concern.

Within a few days, I had appointments with a cardiology specialist and an obstetrician specialist who were brought in to consult on my case. Both described the high risks of my pregnancy. The obstetrician asked if it was worth risking my life for another baby when I already had five young children. And both specialists made it clear that they couldn't guarantee my safety throughout the pregnancy and delivery, or rule out another heart attack, which, according to the statistics of heart attacks like mine, would very likely be fatal. Termination of the pregnancy was suggested.

I cannot describe the range of emotions my husband George and I went through over the next two months. We believed that God was the author of every pregnancy and of every child born, but I was fearful for my life and for my children and understood I could die during the pregnancy or birth if we moved forward.

I turned to the Lord in desperate prayer. As I did, He gave me the key to my situation and said, "Give up the worry about preserving your own life." Having understood His path for me, I simply prayed and committed my life and the growing child within me into His hands. Immediately, I felt relief from my fears, as if a heavy weight had been lifted from me. George and I informed the doctors that we would not terminate but proceed with the pregnancy. We both felt comforted that this was the right choice for us.

Some days later, the Lord showed me a vision while I was praying. I saw the child in my womb being held in His hands. Another time, He told me, "You won't carry this baby." I thought that was strange and I didn't understand what it meant, but as the pregnancy progressed, I noticed a difference between this pregnancy and my previous pregnancies. There was no serious morning sickness. That was a big change! I wasn't exhausted all the time and felt better than I had in ages. I often told George that I didn't even feel like I was pregnant. It was true, the Lord was carrying this baby. There were times along the way when I felt fear, but each time I cried out to the Lord, and my anxieties were soothed and my heart was steadied.

As the months passed, the condition of my heart was an issue raised again by the doctors who were deciding exactly when they should take the baby by cesarean section. They were trying to figure out how I could have the baby and put the least amount of strain on my heart. I was sent to have a heart echo when I was seven months pregnant. The results were amazing. Once damaged, the heart stays damaged and on previous tests my heart had clearly shown the previous damage done by the heart attack. But now the heart echo showed no trace of damage. My husband and I were dumbfounded, and knew that God had performed an incredible miracle. Because of this positive report, the doctors decided to let me go full term and to have a normal delivery.

When the time came to deliver the baby, I hesitated, wondering if I could do this. I worried that something would go wrong with my heart as I pushed. But then, suddenly, a tangible peace overcame my anxiety and settled over both me and George. It was just as if a comforting blanket had been placed over us. It was the presence of God, bringing us reassurance, and we both felt it. I knew in that moment I could push and that everything would be fine. I pushed with the confidence God's peace brought me, and baby Moses was born only two minutes later.

Three weeks after Moses was born, I had an ECG done in the doctor's office. The doctor studied the results very carefully and announced with amazement that the damage had reversed since the heart attack and that my heart had returned to normal. We went on our way, rejoicing and giving thanks that God had taken up the burden we had given Him. He brought our precious miracle baby Moses and me safely through the ordeal. He carried Moses for me.

When Karen and George prayed for an answer and felt that it was the right thing to do to move forward with the pregnancy, the answer they received required great faith and trust in God. Each of us has the same opportunity to ask what is right for us in any situation and to receive our own personal answer. God can heal our physical, emotional, and spiritual wounds, and can carry us safely to the lives we were meant to live. Great miracles can be performed and our faith can be strengthened. The small mercies that can bless every day of our lives can be seen and experienced more fully when we let go and let God.

Choosing to Be Whole

WE ALL HAVE PLACES WHERE WE ARE BROKEN, and we all have problems and are imperfect in many ways. The question is whether we want to hold onto our damage or decide we want to do whatever we can to be whole. It might seem easier to live in the past and to become attached to being a victim. But, if we face our present reality and decide to change, we can invite God to help us become whole and can live a life filled with joy.

It may be that our present reality is so painful that, even though we know intellectually that we need to change, we just can't find the will or the strength to do so. Another block to our progress may be that we do not have the life-skills to change, or the knowledge about how to change. I understand that, at times, it can feel better to just pull the drapes closed and pull the covers over your head and go to sleep. I know what that's like because I've been there. Choosing to be whole is hard work and has to be something we want badly before we will undertake the difficult challenges required by change. We are all children of God – with our wounds, limitations, and difficulties. The question is whether we want to be attached to our hurts, or use them as stepping stones to a better life.

God's Plan for Your Life

The fear of the unknown can keep us clinging to what isn't working for us. It's an act of faith to inquire about God's plan for your life and then follow through to create the life you were meant to live. The payoffs of growth and change include living in the moment, being free of the past, and no longer being controlled or limited by what has come before. Another payoff is that no matter what mistakes we have made in the past, once we decide we want a fresh start, a new life can come to us. We need to exercise faith in God and in the power of the Holy

Spirit to make us whole and to support us in moving on.

Each of us can experience a life full of meaning, a life of worth, and a prosperous life. The new habits that replace old, bad habits are an important part of living a better life, and the rituals and symbols we bring into our life are also important. But the key to our deepest success is found in making a heart-connection with God. For me, this comes from reading the scriptures every day, praying each morning and just before sleep, keeping my focus on the good I'm working to create, and listening in the quiet to hear what God has to say. I encourage you to read the great teachers, explore the wisdom traditions, and read the poetry and inspirational works that will support your growth.

The Old Testament tells the story of the courage Abraham demonstrated. Remember, too, the faith of Joshua sending spies over to see the land God had promised. When one group came back, they said they had seen the land and it was beautiful and rich, but that there was a major obstacle to claiming the birthright. There were giants in the land. Another group said they had seen the beautiful land and had also seen that there were giants in the land, but they expressed faith that with God's help they could claim it.

This belief that we can successfully address our problems with God's help is at the core of living a whole life. Hear God calling your name and reassuring you that you are not alone. Know that you have not been forgotten. If you have doubts, call out to God and ask Him to call your name, so that you can feel the connection to the Divine and have renewed faith.

Deciding To Move Forward

Of all of the books you could be reading right now, this is the one you hold in your hands. As you look at where you are stuck and what holds you back from living the life you were meant to live, ask yourself what you can do in order to become whole, and then make sure you really do want to move forward into greater health, happiness, and prosperity. Decide you want to experience everyday grace and miracles and you will see them at work in your life. What are your challenges and how can God help you overcome them? The Reverend Dr. Lori Cardona found a new beginning in what might have been the end of her life.

Metanoia is a pretty word that has its origin in Greek, meaning "to change." While many of us resist life's difficult transitions, there was a time in my life when I was literally dying for a change.

A long-term relationship had ended and I was suffering the pain of the breakup. Licking my wounds and lamenting my mistakes, I wanted someone to rescue me, to relieve my angst and shame, and to free me from a sense of desperation. I felt as though I had been split in two. I was falling apart, burning down to my ashes, and headed at high speed toward total self-destruction.

At work – when I could get there – I would close my office door and search for an excuse to leave. One day, while sitting at my desk trying desperately to focus, I passed out from not having eaten in several days. An employee found me and had arranged for me to be taken to the hospital where they diagnosed me as being malnourished and depressed. Since I served as the administrator of a mental health clinic, the irony of my predicament was quite amazing.

I was familiar with the term "passive suicide" and knew that it described my situation. I was wasting away in my despair, having lost over twenty-five pounds from what was an already thin body. I hadn't eaten solid food in close to a month, and now agoraphobia kept me from leaving the house for more that a few miles and a few minutes at a time. My depression became debilitating, keeping me indoors and under covers for up to three to four days at a time.

I was severely sleep-deprived and every night, throughout the night, I would lie in bed, stare out into the darkness, and write suicide letters in my head. I planned what I would do to end my life but didn't have the strength to get up and write it all down. The idea that I fixated on was that I would call a friend who lived several miles away from my home. I would ask her to come by sometime in the evening. When she arrived I would already be dead. I would leave the front door open and have a note for her set out on the dining room table, advising her to call for assistance and not to come into the bedroom because my dead body would be there. In the note, I would list names of people for her to call, and would ask her to say that I had died of a heart attack so that it would be easer for them to handle the news of my death. I would tell her who to call to take care of my bird and my cat. I would have the names and numbers listed in no particular order of priority.

Thinking back, I realize that I was functioning in the delusional thinking common in a major depression. But, during those agonizing nights, I thought my ideas for ending my life were brilliant. I would escape the emotional pain that was keeping me from food, work, friends, and life. It was the only thing that made sense to me. In those dark nights, all I wanted was the strength to carry out my plan. In the day, I walked through a cloud of confusion and foggy thoughts, barely capable of making conversation.

One day at work, I heard screaming in the hallway. A man had come into our building who was clearly having a psychotic breakdown and it was clear that he might be dangerous. Someone had called the police and everyone had cleared the lobby. I got up from my desk and slowly walked down the hall to speak with him. He turned his head and watched as I approached, all the while continuing his stream of profanities and his frantic, desperate tirade. My staff tried to stop me, implored me to stay away from him. But there was something in his eyes, something I understood because I felt it myself. As we stood facing each other he asked, "Do you know who I am?" I shook my head to indicate that, no, I did not know who he was. He told me things I knew weren't true, but that he, in his madness, believed. He was the son of the president, he told me, the grandson of a king, and as he ran down his list of delusions, I listened. There was only one difference between us – I was not screaming out loud.

Then, on a particularly bleak night, my phone rang at two in the morning. The caller was a stranger to me, but was someone who knew a friend of a friend of mine. She had called to tell me what a horrible person I was. She told me that I was a worthless human being and the volume and intensity of her voice increased every time I tried to interrupt her barrage of insults.

She cursed at me, called me names, told me that I was no good, and even wondered aloud why I was alive. I became very quiet and focused on what she had to say. I was filled with self-loathing and I wanted to hear all the unkindness she wanted to spew. In my heart, I agreed with her. Her tirade gave me the strength to finally carry out my plan for relief and for a final escape.

It takes only a moment to lose the natural instinct for survival. And, in that moment, I decided I was ready to die. I could see no future and had no hope. I hung up the phone, got up from my bed, and shook off the depression's exhausting restraint. I walked to the kitchen and pulled out the blender. I poured two can of a vitamin-rich chocolate drink, the food that had kept me going when I lost my appetite. I added the contents of four different prescription medications, a variety of anti-depressants and anti-anxiety trial medications, and for good measure, I added two bottles of sleeping pills.

The sound of the blender chewing through the pills was eerily comforting. I had to rest my head against the cold glass of the counter top when I turned off the blender. I was so tired. I went to the sofa and took a short nap, then got up as if in a trance, returning to the kitchen for another look at my concoction. I decided to prepare my body for its death by lighting a ceremonial smudging stick of sage. I wasn't sure what to do with it, so I just stood holding it as it burned. I found it hard to breathe, to think, to move. I was paralyzed in my grief. I decided not to write the letter to my friend after all. It seemed too difficult, to complex, too tiring. I was ready to just get it over with.

I poured the poison into a glass and took a sip. By now the sun was beginning to rise. I held the glass to my mouth. And then, the phone rang. At first, I ignored it. But it rang again and again and again. For some reason, the voice mail system didn't pick up. It seemed as if the ringing was getting louder and screaming out my name. Finally, I threw the glass in the sink, ran across the room, and cried out into the phone to whoever was there. What followed were a series of Divine interventions. God sent friends, teachers, preachers, books, and all of the support I needed to deeply change from the inside out, to shift my mind and heart from hopelessness to faith and trust. I finally became motivated to participate in my healing and I learned to move my thinking from an ego-centered focus on my misery to an intense, internal, spiritual focus that invited God to help make me whole.

In the end, the death I experienced was not of my literal body, but of an old self, an old way of thinking and being. I found my direction, my spiritual path, and I learned new ways to address and correct my areas of weakness. I looked at my life with rigorous honestly, and I crafted a new life with God. I made a solemn commitment to make real and permanent change. Metanoia. Change. It was not easy, but it was necessary, and the change was the greatest blessing of my life. Thank you, God, for my miraculous new life in You.

A Wakeup Call

Lori took on the need to change at a deep spiritual level when she sunk as low as she could go without killing herself. Terri Tiffany shares her story of coming to the brink of surrender with a scare that shook her at the foundations and grounded her life in new faith.

I received a phone call from the radiology department that was scheduled to perform two biopsies on my left breast. Juggling my bag of groceries, I reached for the cell phone my daughter was holding. "Mrs. Tiffany, this clinic is 'out of network' and your procedure tomorrow will cost you over two-thousand dollars and possibly more, should there be any complications."

I had waited for this appointment for a long time, and now I would have to wait even longer. My only option was to start over and find a doctor who would take my insurance. I glanced at my daughter and measured her troubled look. "There must be a reason. We'll just have to wait." I didn't believe my words for a second. I could not stand the fear, and understanding that this period of not knowing was going to be extended was very hard. I tried to project hope to my family and friends and act as if my life was normal, but of course, it wasn't.

I needed time alone to assemble my thoughts, but there was so much to do that I didn't take the time I needed to get grounded. Since the biopsies had been cancelled, I needed to get my x-rays to another doctor.

The drive to the mammogram facility took me back to the same parking lot where days earlier I had called my best friend and shared my darkest fears. I had hoped and prayed that by this day, I would be calling to rejoice with good news. I tried to convince everyone around me of my inner strength. "I'm healthy. I'm young. Don't worry. Lots of women go through this." I kissed the wrinkle on my husband's forehead.

As the clock ticked past the originally scheduled time for my surgery, unexpected tears flowed. All I knew was that I had three areas of noteworthy concern in my left breast, and that the doctor had described what he saw on the x-ray as unlike anything he had ever seen. Now I was in the waiting room again and women of all ages sat in hospital gowns facing each of their individual fears about what might be discovered. I found it increasingly hard to breathe.

I read my Bible, searching in vain for a scripture that would soothe me. I separated each page, reading scripture after scripture. "Where are you, great Physician?" My heart whispered, desperately needing His comfort. The answer came through the mail. On this day there were no piles of unwanted junk mail, just one lone card from a dear friend. I peeled back the flap and smiled at two mice merrily hugging one another. Beneath the illustration she had written, *Philippians 4:6, 7. I read aloud the promise delivered to me as a Divine grace. Do not be anxious about anything, but in everything by prayer and petition with thanksgiving present your requests to God. And the peace of God which transcends all understanding will guard your hearts and your minds in Christ Jesus.*

The card had arrived at my lowest point, and the words gave me great comfort. He understood the burden of my anxiety and renewed His promise to care for me. I felt assured that the next step forward would be taken with God. His arms would be there to carry me.

Forty-four days and three procedures later, I was ushered into my surgeon's tidy office. I carried God's words in my heart along with my hope. Since the day God renewed my faith, I knew I was ready to accept any news the doctor might deliver and that I could surrender to

God's will for me. I held my breath as he opened my chart and turned to speak the words that would set me free. "There's no cancer. There aren't even pre-cancerous cells. You're fine." God walked into the office with me, and He walked out with me, and my life was changed.

The strength Terri showed by surrendering to God's will for her life, and then rejoicing in her good health is a reminder of how important it is to let our traumas pass once they are finished. She moved on with her productive and healthy life with a renewed sense of faith, and her life was blessed.

Feeding the Good

I remember hearing the Reverend James Trapp, President and CEO of the Association of Unity Churches speak about letting go of our suffering. He said that some of us needed to get off the cross because others needed the wood. In my work, I truly understand the healing power of telling our stories to each other, and there may be great value in retelling them numerous times. But, if we hold on too tightly to our pain and continue to relive it over and over again, we continue to reinforce our anxiety and this adds to our stress. Our brain reacts to things we imagine or fear, and to bad experiences we relive again as if they are happening in that very moment. Our body reads thoughts as being experience rather than just thoughts.

My encouragement is to bring attention to what you think about and to share your dark times with others with authenticity, but to do so with the conscious intention of moving into the light. What we focus on, we feed upon, and we are what we eat, after all. With God's help, we can let the past be the past and can move into a healthier present and a glorious future. When we are finished with the past, we are free to feel the good we find in the present moment.

Food For The Soul

For me, this feeding of body and spirit also extends to the ritual of eating well as a part of living well. I love living on Miami Beach in Florida, or what we locals call South Beach. Living on South Beach means that I have wonderful food close at hand, and I am also truly blessed to live near one of the finest chefs on South Beach, Stefano LaCava. As I talked to him about this book and its focus on everyday grace, we both immediately thought of including food, since we both believe it is an important part of living a spiritual life. The choice to be whole includes what we put in our bodies and how we treat them every day. It seems to me that our spiritual, emotional, and mental health are so closely tied to our physical health, that we benefit from taking our entire health into account as we make decisions about how to live a Godly life.

My love for food runs very deep and my appreciation for eating good food is grounded in an appreciation for life, and for what God has provided me. We have to eat in order to live, and I believe that bringing careful attention to what we eat is a spiritual meditation. Food gives me pure joy and increases my appreciation for all good things. I tend to remember people and places in terms of the food we enjoyed together and the feeling of the place and what the food was like. I explore the cultures of the world though their wonderful food, and feel an increased appreciation for my brothers and sisters as a result.

I love to taste different flavors exploding in my mouth. I love to focus on the texture and enjoy seeing the colors of the food. I particularly love it when the natural flavor of foods comes through. I also like the sense of community I feel when I return to the same place to get my food. I return often to the Diana Café, a small Cuban restaurant in downtown Miami. When I stop by I always say, "Quiero una empanada de pollo, y un jugo de naranja sin yielo, por favor." And my chicken empanada and orange juice without ice is the perfect thing. Sometimes I eat it in the café, and at other times I eat this treat as I walk to my car, enjoying every morsel. This kind of ritual feels as rich to me as any of the other self-care I attend to in my life.

When I was having such a tough time financially, I used my love of food to help fuel the changes I needed to make in my life. I used my passion for food to help me succeed in turning things around. I dreamed of sitting in the restaurants I wanted to visit and imagined traveling to the places I wanted to see, and then I worked to get back to wholeness because I missed that part of my life so much.

Food is truly a part of my heart and soul. What is it that gives your life great pleasure? What helps you feel whole and full of the joy of being alive? Knowing who you are, and what you have the potential to become, will help you understand how to feed your soul. God wants us to experience joy and cheers us on as we learn how to live more fully and with greater appreciation for all that is good. Chef Stefano LaCava has experienced times when he felt that life had let him down, times when he worried that his demons would take over his life and he wouldn't get it back. He was in the middle of a dark time when he received a phone call that would transform a bleak time into a wonderful summer that blessed his life.

After living in paradise for several years, literally living on Paradise Island and Harbor Island, in the Bahamas, I passed up a job in Beijing at the Sheraton Great Wall of China because I realized that Florida could be a place to see my dreams come true. I wanted to make my parents happy and to settle down and have a family. I wanted to be near my grandparents – my grandfather Stefano, who was ill, and Jennie, the grandmother who had raised me and with whom I share a deep spiritual connection.

When I moved to South Florida, I got married, opened a restaurant and my wife and I had a child all within one year. Things seemed perfect, but then a very dark time arrived and I lost my job, the marriage ended, and I found myself in a custody battle for our adopted child. I was sleeping on the couch in my grandmother's house and my life was full of lawyers and judges and financial stress. I thought things had spiraled down so far that I wouldn't be able to turn my life around.

One day the phone rang, and I was asked to get on a plane to Telluride, Colorado to cook for Oprah Winfrey and her guests and staff. She was building a new home in the San Juan Mountains, near Ralph Lauren's ranch and Sylvester Stallone's Hideout in Heaven. Oprah needed me to cook for her under the special guidelines that would support her health and weight loss, but most importantly, she wanted to treat her guests and staff to something special. It was quite a challenge for me to cook at 7,000 feet above sea level. I was used to cooking at sea level and this was high-altitude cooking where water does not boil at the same temperature, oxygen is thin, and getting food to do what I wanted it to do was much harder than I expected. I accepted the mission, knowing my life was in ruins in Florida. Oprah was a Seraphim in my life, the highest form of an angel. She is truly special and is greatly loved for good reason. She takes a sincere personal interest in everyone's life and she shared her spiritual and life advice with me. I felt supported during my time cooking for her and so I share these recipes because they were inspired by the angels around me that summer in Telluride. It was a summer that changed my life for the better.

All of these recipes are easy and simple, and can help you enjoy eating the healthy food that also feeds the soul. I created these recipes for use on grilled or steamed fish such as mahi mahi, sea bass, fresh water perch, halibut or salmon.

Seasoned and Infused Vinegars

USE FRESH, OR BOTTLE AND USE AFTER REFRIGERATION

Orange Joy

1 cup champagne vinegar

1 tsp orange zest

1 juice of whole orange

2 tbsp grape seed oil

1 tsp fresh rosemary (chopped)

Shitaki Essence

1 cup tamari (Deep Sea Soy)

1 cup honey

6 Shitaki mushrooms sliced thin (raw)

1 pc star anise

1 pinch black pepper

Asian Lemon Grass

1 tsp lemon grass

1 cup rice wine vinegar

4 tsp sesame oil

1 tsp cardamon seeds (ground)

1 tsp pickled ginger

1 small red chili

Italian Balsamic Basil

1 cup balsamic vinegar (Modena)

1 cup red wine vinegar

2 whole garlic cloves

1 tbsp chopped basil

2 tbsp olive oil

1 pinch red pepper (crushed)

Honoring His Creation

Our Creator gave us bodies that need food, water, sleep and exercise in order to function well. It is my strong sense that we can make each of these activities a tribute to our creator by preparing and eating wonderful food with gusto, drinking pure water with enjoyment, sleeping the hours we need in order to feel properly rested, and exercising and caring for our body in ways that demonstrate that we honor God's creation. Self-respect, self-love and self-care show that we have a reverence for life and that we desire wholeness and health. When I talk to women and men about health, I often hear things from them that make me worry that as a culture we confuse being skinny with being healthy. God made us in many shapes and sizes, and if we don't honor that important fact, we miss the point that the human family is not one-size-fits-all. The goal is not to be skinny and to try any fad diet or pill that might do damage to our body as we suffer to squeeze it into an unrealistic shape. Our job of being good stewards of our body is to be healthy, self-accepting, and to take great care of the body that comes to us from our genetic history and as a gift from God.

Every body needs a balanced diet with fresh fruits and vegetables every day, good water to hydrate us properly, and exercise and adequate rest. Most people don't get enough sleep and that has all sorts of negative consequences. We need energy to be whole. Rest is a priority, not a luxury.

Like most of us, I have had a problem with the subject of exercise. I had taken care of myself for a time, but when my life took a nose dive, I stopped exercising. I'm not sure which came first. Did I stop exercising and then lose control of my life, or did I lose control of my life and also lose the energy to exercise? It's that chicken and egg question. The worse I felt, the less I did physically and the less attention I paid to my body, the worse I felt.

Now I have found the kind of exercise that feeds my soul and cares for my body – I walk. I try to walk as much as I can. I walk up stairs, I park a distance from my destination and walk. I walk to do errands, but most of all, I walk for fun. I have found that the book *Tune-Up* by Sandi Morais is very helpful because it is simple and easy to follow, and some days I go to the beach and just walk and walk. I love to see and hear the water and to be near it. My soul is fed by the activity and my body rejoices.

If you haven't found the way to exercise that suits your soul best, keep experimenting until you find what works for you and then do it regularly. We all need to walk, work out, swim, play ball, jog, dance, do yoga, Pilates, or something that keeps us fit and our bodies well cared for. It is interesting to me that the thing we can do to best protect our bodies against disease, and to support ourselves in aging gracefully, is to do with consciousness and attention the very things God designed our bodies to need. He gave us the body, but we are in charge of maintenance.

Living In The Now

: Chapter Thirteen

HARD TIMES DON'T LAST FOREVER, but they can feel as if they will go on without end, unless we let our troubles surface and move out of our lives gently. It is easy to experience the weight of difficulties as being even harder than they are if we become too attached to our challenges. What can we do to avoid spiraling down into a dark place? How can we be careful not to miss the blessings that can be found right under our nose?

I know from experience how easily I can overlook blessings or not appreciate them fully when I am not living in the present moment. It's so easy to be stuck in the past, or to live into projections about the future. When we decide to live in the "now" we can accept the curve balls life throws us with more grace. Focusing on the present moment, we can feel exactly what we feel right now, but not add the burden of how terrible things might be in the future, or how challenging they were in the past.

Live This Day

In order to experience everyday grace and miracles, simply concentrate on appreciating both the blessings and the challenges that are before you on just this single day. Where are you right now? Name the things for which you can be grateful – today. And name the challenges you face – today. You can take things one day at a time in order to shrink your concerns into a more manageable framework. And you can give thanks for what is working well in your life in this moment.

I believe it is important to do everything I can today – and then leave the rest to God. Living the life you were meant to live can start in this moment, and not in some far off time when everything aligns perfectly. By taking small steps to make your life more fulfilling now, you can experience progress within the cycle of even in a single day. When you live in and love the present, you have complete access to the joy of being alive.

Grace Boneschansker shares a story that illustrates the spiritual truth that in death we are in the midst of life and that in life there is also death. Her ability to live in the moment sets her free to connect with the Divine even during a difficult time.

Over ten years ago, my husband and I purchased a two-unit apartment building to be used predominantly for ministry. We've housed an ex-street person, a Tanzanian missionary family, and a disabled woman, offering all of them a real home. What our building needed was a garden – a perennial one to symbolize the power of the resurrection. I planted the garden in faith and prayed it would take hold. Every fall, the plants would wither and "die," but in the spring, the flowers would come to life in splendor.

My mother had particularly beautiful peonies in her garden and they seemed to symbolize my mother in some way. I was thrilled when she gave me a cutting to put in my own garden and I placed it right in the center, hoping it would become the showpiece of the garden. I then waited patiently for something to happen. For the first couple of years, nothing did. I would watch in eager anticipation in early May as the leaves of the peony stretched out of the ground, grew and then eventually withered in September without having produced a blossom.

Then, our family was hit with a bombshell. My mother had colon cancer, and her oncologist believed she would probably be gone within two years. I couldn't believe it. My mother, Japanese in origin, ate only healthy meals of stir-fried vegetables, didn't smoke, and exercised regularly. I couldn't believe she could be facing death so young. She was only sixty-four. My brothers and I were losing a mother, my children their "Bachian," my father his beloved wife, my husband, his doting mother-in-law, and my grandmother, her daughter. I forgot about my garden for a time and concentrated on taking care of my mother.

Watching a loved one slowly die is excruciating, especially towards the end. I found myself switching roles with her, taking care of her as she once had taken care of me. My dad was in his seventies and also in failing health, and I had two young daughters I was trying to guide through adolescence. My emotions ran from anger with God to discouragement, fear, and then inconsolable grief. As I took every day as it came, I also experienced the most intimate experiences I had ever had with God. There were many times when I could feel His loving arms around us all. I had a supportive Bible study group who prayed for our family, and they lifted us up just by their presence in our lives.

As predicted, two years later my mother passed away. I wanted to know that I would see my mother again and I wanted to have faith that her spirit was fine. I returned to tending my overgrown and neglected garden the following spring, and, as usual, the peony sprouted leaves. Soon, tiny buds started to appear. This was nothing new, they previously would come out, stay the same size, and then die back without blooming. However, during the next week, the buds grew bigger, and after another couple of weeks, they blossomed. Six exquisite, crimson peonies graced the centre of my garden! I was so overcome with emotion that I fell to my knees and wept with joy, heedless of anyone who might see me. "Yes," I sensed God speaking to me, "you will see your beloved mother again."

Survive and Thrive

In my own struggles, and in my work with others, I have found three simple ways to not just endure a difficult time, but to turn it into an opportunity to learn how to be more resilient and understand how to thrive.

1. Limit the scope. No matter what you are dealing with, take on only what you need to cope with in the moment. If you are having a health challenge, focus on that and let an issue that is pending with your career or relationship wait until the health problem has passed. In other words, don't overload what you need to deal with unnecessarily by projecting one complication into other areas of your life. Take big issues on one at a time and one day at a time.

2. Keep your focus on the present. If you project the worst of what is currently happening into the future and imagine that things will continue to get worse, you'll feel the weight of more negativity than you can cope with right now. Suffer what you need to suffer in the moment, but don't add dark imaginings on top of it.

3. Use this time well. Times of trial are often the most transformative and meaningful times in our lives. Look for the lessons you can learn from your difficulties, and see problems as ways of expanding your awareness of life, learning greater compassion for others, and connecting with God. The refining fire of a difficult time can help you build a better life.

Angalete Dye is someone who has focused first on surviving, and is now expanding her life in order to thrive. She has faced enormous challenges, but she decided to grow beyond them in order to build a better life.

Being a single-mother can be overwhelming – it seems to always be about struggling in one way or another. Mentally and physically, I get so drained, and can sometimes feel as if my faith is being tested daily. I've got two beautiful children, sixteen month-old Sali'yah, and four year-old Ari'ana, and I work full-time as a substitute teacher for a local high school in Miramar, Florida. I thank God for my time with my daughters and for our many blessings. We've been through some very hard times but I have relied on the testimonies of others to help build myself up and get to a better place. I have learned to ask God to guide me every day.

I went from being a "church girl" on a full-ride college basketball scholarship, to being alone with two children, depressed, and extremely stressed. When I had my first daughter, I was very dependant on my baby's father, because he was the only family I had. Throughout our relationship, we dealt with so many of his demons, but he just couldn't get a handle on money, drugs, women, work, and a list of problems that never ended. The drama was just too much for me, but I hung in as long as I could. We would break up and make up and I came up pregnant again. I found myself in an abusive relationship, I had a two year-old to support, a job that barely made ends meet, and now I was pregnant again. My first thought was abortion because I was sure I could not afford another baby or raise another child on my own. At this point, I prayed to God asking him to please miraculously make me not pregnant, or send a sign, or a messenger of some kind.

I went to work campaigning for a politician and was assigned to pass out flyers with two other ladies. We talked as we worked and gradually I began to feel comfortable with them. I decided to ask their advice, indirectly. "I have a friend who is pregnant and who has a young child already. What would you tell her?"

The first woman, who was high in energy and spirit said, "Tell that girl to have her baby! The Lord is not going to put more on her than she can bear. I'm raising my drug-addicted sister's five year-old daughter, and I've been living with AIDS for seven years. Sometimes, I'm in so much pain I can't get out of bed to care for her. I pray, and the Lord answers me by giving her the wisdom to understand the situation, and me the strength I need. Usually, I can get up and do what I have to do by God's grace. So tell her to keep her baby and pray. Leave it in the Lord's hands, have faith in him."

I was in awe of how much she was coping with and her huge faith. The other woman also responded enthusiastically. "Amen! Tell her that her kids will always be hers. I've got ten children and I've been stabbed, raped, and abused physically and mentally, I jumped out a two-story window trying to get away from a man I was with, and I've hidden for months with little or no support for my kids. You know, sometimes things just don't work out, but the Lord blessed me with all of my kids and I love them. I struggle, and with constant prayer, the Lord sees me through. So, tell your friend to stand firm and trust and believe in the Lord. Tell her that He will direct her path and shield her from danger. Tell her to go to church and to pray."

These two strong women stood in front of me, testifying that God could see any of us through any obstacle. For the rest of the day, we ministered to one another, and as I left work I cried and prayed all the way home. I had an answer from God. He had sent two helpful messengers to me. That night, I got on the phone proudly to spread my news that I was expecting another baby.

I still struggle, but now I have stronger faith and I've learned to become a prayer warrior. With every situation, I pray my way through, knowing that God answers all prayers in the timeframe and in the way He sees fit. I'm not perfect, but I am determined to live right. With God, there is always a solution. I stay prayed up, and I step out in faith.

Living in Awe

When we focus on the "now," we have a heightened sense of being, and we experience things more keenly. It seems important to take pleasure where we can find it and to make sure we are noticing the beauty of the rainbow, the kindness of others, and the many blessings that surround us. I try to stay in touch with this feeling of awe because it is a way to connect with God. Imagine if we could live with the enthusiasm and excitement of children discovering the wonders of the world. When I lived in England, studying to be a midwife, I was in a classroom when I saw snow for the first time. The instructor casually mentioned that it was snowing outside, and I jumped up in the middle of the class and ran to the window in awe. She was used to snow, but I found snow to be a miracle.

I know there are many undiscovered opportunities to notice the miracles around us, and to enjoy the small things more than we do. What awakens a sense of awe in you, and how can you find it more often? When I feel I am not living in the present, I try to experience a small detail that I'm missing in order to ground me in the moment again. If I'm troubled and not falling asleep, I feel the clean cool sheet and concentrate on appreciating that simple pleasure. This awareness brings me back to the moment, which allows me to feel the peace of knowing that tomorrow will take care of itself.

Mustard Seed Faith

BEING CARRIED ON WINGS OF FAITH is one of the best feelings I know, but faith is a complicated thing and it seems as if faith and doubt tend to work together. It is probably impossible for any of us to live in total faith, but I've learned that some doubt is acceptable as well. When we try so hard to believe, at some level we know we're trying too hard that that we don't really have faith. We cannot try to have faith, we learn to have faith and with practice and experience our faith becomes stronger and deeper.

I was curious about the kind of faith it would take to move mountains, and so I picked up a package of mustard seeds and pasted just one seed on a postcard and put it where I could see it every day. When I face great doubt, all I need to do is find faith the size of that mustard seed with which to counter that doubt. This encourages me greatly, because a mustard seed is very tiny.

Growing Wings of Faith

I have felt more faith developing in me as I have learned to bring compassion to myself and understand that I don't have to be perfectly stalwart. I only have to continue to plant the seed of faith and let it grow. When I work with people, I call it "growing your faith wings," because nothing builds faith like faith. Karen Reno Knapp shares a story of her four children finding their own little budding wings of faith.

> It was a hot day, and our family was taking our first real vacation in a long time. We needed this break and things were going all right, except that my husband John had hurt his back, we had run into rainstorms, and our car brakes needed repair, and so we were running behind

schedule. When I finally remembered to call our motel for the night to confirm our reservation, I found I was ten minutes late and that they had given our room away. Nine year-old Eli, who tends to be a worrier inquired, "What will we do? It's late and we'll never find a motel." We drove on in edgy silence. After carefully considering things Eli spoke up again, "Let's pray that God will help us." I asked him to offer the prayer for our family and as soon as he said, "Amen," he added, "But God doesn't answer my prayers."

Like an echo, his older brother Ethan responded, "God doesn't answer my prayers either."

Eleven year-old Phoebe chimed in, "God doesn't answer my prayers."

And her little brother five year-old Andrew joined the refrain with a loud, "God doesn't answer my prayers, either."

I gave them a lecture about how God hears and answers all of our prayers but not always exactly how and when we want, but they didn't seem convinced.

Around bedtime, we stumbled upon a row of motels. Our hopes rose but only briefly. As the children and I waited in the car, my husband John returned from each motel dejected. One motel had one room available but it was too expensive for us. No other rooms were available. As I noticed the "No Vacancy" signs up and down the street, I couldn't help but think of another weary family traveling to Bethlehem. They didn't have a reservation either and God had provided a place for them. I hoped He would do the same for us.

John tried one more motel and this time they had a small room with a pull-out bed that could work if the kids squeezed in with their sleeping bags. We could have it for a price we could afford and it included a continental breakfast in the morning. Ecstatic, Eli and the others raced up to the room. The room was connected to a giant conference room that we could use on the condition that we didn't "bother anything." We had, in essence, a two-room suite with plenty of room. When it was time for the children to say their prayers John said, "What were you all saying about God not answering your prayers?" Our prayers were prayers of gratitude that night and, as I drifted off to sleep, I identified with two weary travelers of long ago who found shelter in a stable. The world may have changed a great deal since them, but God has not. He still hears and answers our prayers.

In order to grow your faith wings I encourage you to pray not only for small things, but to set aside some time every month and take on something you worry might be impossible and ask God to help you make it possible. You might model this prayer of faith like the Lord's prayer, and begin by thanking God for His many blessings. This prepares you to put your faith in action because you will be freshly reminded that you are truly blessed and that there is much to be thankful for. Then, pray for the help and guidance to know what is best for your life, and ask God to assist you in making the impossible possible.

Tonie-Beth Vernon is fourteen years-old and lives in Jamaica. She has started to grow her wings of faith and offers her story of how fasting and prayer can change things.

My family and I were supposed to go abroad to visit my auntie and cousins in Canada for the summer. However, this soon seemed like an impossibility when the travel agency called to let us know our flight would have to be postponed because the embassy was taking too long with our visas.

I was at my daddy's office when his secretary told me the bad news. I felt that this trip was very important to our family, so I told my daddy's secretary that I was going to fast and pray. She joined me in my prayer, which I appreciated very much. The visas came through two days before we were scheduled to leave. My daddy explained that when his secretary called the embassy, she managed to get through to one of the counselors. This was not supposed to happen because the phone system doesn't allow anyone to get through to a counselor. When the secretary called, the counselor asked her how she got the special number. The secretary explained that she had just followed the automated system and that this is where she ended up. The counselor pulled the file and prepared the visas. My Auntie Veronica called to say it was the fasting and prayer that caused God to tap into the phone system to make it happen this way.

This experience helped me realize that when you set your mind to something, it can happen, according to God's will. Today, my family jokes with me saying they should come to me with their problems so I can fast and pray for them. If a girl like me can fast and pray and have God listen, so can anybody.

It's a wonderful thing to see children building their faith at a young age. Valora Otis and her family also experienced the faith that comes "out of the mouths of babes" when they turned to God for an everyday miracle.

"Val, I just had the strongest feeling that I should have taken that last exit," my husband Terry said, while running his fingers through his hair. Our four boys were quiet.

"Just take the next one." I answered. We were all anxious because we had hit a skunk the previous day and the van reeked of the spray and so did we. The skunk had run in front of us and Terry swerved trying to miss the poor thing, but it was unavoidable. It was disconcerting not to know if we had killed the skunk, and we were still jumpy from the experience in the way people are after an accident of any kind.

I was amazed that the hotel manager had let us into our rooms that night. The aroma of six skunked travelers was enough to make a grown man weep. We tried to park as far as possible from the hotel so that the smell wouldn't upset anyone, and now we had been back on the road again for an entire day and the sun was setting.

We doubled back to find our exit, and then we heard the van suddenly decelerate. As we crossed the overpass, the loud sound of pieces of the engine clacking loudly exploded from under the hood.
"The oil pressure just bottomed out." Terry growled. We sat by the side of the road in a silence so complete it made my gut ache. The cell

phone was dead, the car was dead, and it was dark. Then our young son Hunter spoke up, "Father in Heaven knows where we are and he will send help if we ask him." He pleaded, "Let's say a family prayer."

"Out of the mouths of babes," my husband whispered. Terry gnawed on his bottom lip holding back emotion and he reached out for my hand. In the darkness of a cornfield our family bowed our heads and prayed. We placed our wellbeing in our Father's hands. Three minutes later, the headlights of a lone car appeared. "Mom, look! I knew Heavenly Father would help us!" Hunter beamed.

The boys cheered. My husband kissed me. And we expressed our gratitude that Father heard our prayers for assistance and sent us help. The faith of a child prompted a simple prayer, and our faith as a family grew as a result.

God Will Provide

When my mother talked about a certain kind of powerful faith, she called it "staying faith," meaning the kind of faith that does not falter no matter how hopeless things may appear. She often expressed that sort of faith and would remind her children that even when we could not see God's hand at work, we could always trust God's heart. Pachent Gordon-Smythe has a mother with the same strong faith. Pachent is married with two children and now lives in the Cayman Islands, but she grew up in Jamaica, like I did. Her story of faith in the power of God to provide is a compelling one.

I grew up in the country, the third child of nine – five boys and four girls. We all loved the freshness of the breeze and the lush green plants of our Caribbean island, Jamaica. The hills of Brighton were joyful, and the cool wind helped us do without air conditioning. We had an interesting and lively family life with our potpourri of personalities and we tried to live Godly lives.

Each day started off with a family prayer meeting at 5:30 in the morning, a time cherished by our parents, but not by us because we always wanted a little more sleep. Later in life, we appreciated what we learned during those morning hours, and we remembered Bible verses we studied as children, like the one in Matthew that reminds us to "take no thought for the morrow."

My mother was the district dressmaker and also made all kinds of craft work. My father was a builder who was also good at cabinet making, surveying, and any other trade he could get his hands on. He was a Mr. Fix-it in the district and was even asked to extract a tooth one time. We had some very good times as a family, and our parents taught us the value of waiting on God and of being satisfied with the blessing we had already received.

Sadly, my father died young, leaving Mama with all nine of us, the oldest aged eighteen and the youngest only three. Our world practically caved in without our Papa. A cloud of sorrow hung over our home and there was a vast emptiness in our hearts. We consoled ourselves by revisiting his jokes, retelling his stories, and trying to keep his memory alive.

After his death, our lifestyle changed rapidly, for the worse. Mama was not getting any work, no one purchased her craft items, and many of the customers who owed her money went to someone else for new work without first paying Mama what they owed. We did what farming we could, but our little farm was failing. In spite of our hardships, Mama spoke of God's provision and His help. She was always thankful and believed that God would come through for her. We were not totally convinced, but Mama prayed hard and she always found a way. "God will provide." She said, and help did seem to come. When we needed money, someone came with mending.

One terrible day, all our resources had been used up. There were no more yams or potatoes in the field, the water in the concrete tank was gone, and all the shops had refused to give us credit for food because we could not pay our bills. Customers who owed Mama were not paying her, and this seemed like the end. The little children fussed because they were hungry, and we older children were as brave as we could be. Mama moved by faith and she cried out to the Lord in desperation – the kind we seldom saw and the younger ones couldn't understand.

Habakkuk 3:17-18 came alive in her sewing room as she prayed aloud. *Although the fig tree shall not blossom, neither shall fruit be in the vines; the labor of the olives shall fail, and the fields shall yield no meat; the flock shall be cut off from the fold, and there shall be no herd in the stalls: Yet I will rejoice in the Lord, I will joy in the God of my salvation.*

Mama was desperate, but she continued to rejoice in the Lord. She also reminded Him of His promise to look after the fatherless and the widow. Things were at their very worst when she called out to my brother Ord to put the pot on the fire. We all shared the responsibility of cooking dinner and tonight was his turn. We looked at Mama in amazement because she knew that there was no food in the house!

Ord replied, "Mama, all we have is some wood and water."

"I know son," Mama replied, "but put the pot on, in the name of the Lord." So reluctantly, he put the pot on the fire. While the water heated, Mama prayed. After a couple of minutes, Ord returned to Mama.

"The water is boiling and drying out of the pot and there is no food, Mama."

She said, "Son, put more water in the pot. By the time it boils again, God will have provided us with food!"

Very frustrated, Ord put more water in the pot and more wood on the fire. We were obedient to Mama, but at that time we didn't have faith in what she said. Mama looked sad, but her eyes were filled with hope and belief.

"Children," she said, "we must have faith in God. He promised to help us in times of need and I believe He will. I don't know how, but He is going to provide food. Just be a little more patient." Before she could say another word, a boy called out to us from the gate. "Hello! Sister Linda?"

"Come in!' Mama answered.

"My mother sent this for you," the boy said.

It was a bag filled with breadfruit, yams, and potatoes – payment for a dress our mother had made some time ago. Our eyes widened with surprise because we suddenly had dinner! Before Mama could finish her thank you to the boy, a woman came to our door. "Sister Linda, here's a little piece of meat for your dinner." It was Sister Shaw, Mama's good friend. Her husband was a butcher, and now we had meat.

Mama lifted her hands and praised God for His provisions. Food and meat poured in over the next few days, and we experienced so much abundance that we passed along some food to others we knew who needed it more than we did. We learned that no matter what, God has a way, and that we should never give up! He will come to our rescue during times when we are convinced there is no way out. He is God and His promises are sure! I do my best to use the principles of Mama's faith. Her love for Him strengthens me, and her example helps me exercise faith every day.

This is a good time to think about what you want to work on in faith during this coming month. Take some time to pray about a challenge that is the most important in your life right now and write about it in your journal so that you have a record of where you are now and what you are working to change. Write about your faith, either your small mustard seed of faith, or your larger "staying faith." Focus your attention and ask for God's help for one important thing for a full month, and then look back on what you have written and see where the Lord has taken you. Your faith can move mountains and solve problems, it can open hearts and lead the way to the life you were meant to live. Your faith can create everyday miracles.

Born To Serve

WE SERVE GOD WHEN WE SERVE OTHERS, and although it is easy to understand this concept at an intellectual and spiritual level, it can be hard to implement in practical ways. How do we find the right way to serve that suits our skills and abilities? Who do we serve and when? How can we be sure we are balancing the needs of others with our own needs, so that we don't become depleted by the service we offer. I believe that healthy and God-focused service fills us up and makes us feel closer to God. When I hear about someone offering service that sounds as if it comes from martyrdom, or is discussed with complaining, and whining, I worry that something is seriously out of balance. Our service needs to make us feel energized and connected to our brothers and sisters and to the Divine. Our service needs to make us more whole.

We can find a cure for too much self-focus when we expand our awareness of others and get beyond the concerns of our lives in order to serve others. The golden rule is a perspective that can take on a life of its own, when we take on the challenge to treat everyone like we want to be treated. Everyone? Not just those who are like us, not just those we already like, and those who treat us kindly. We're supposed to love people who are challenging, difficult and unlikable? We know God's answer to that question, and learning to love others like we love ourselves is a task we can focus on our entire lifetime.

Our God is concerned about compassion, and asks us to practice it daily. This is a challenge we cannot ignore if we want to live the life we were meant to live and feel close to God. In order to experience everyday grace and miracles, our hearts have to turn toward service. I have seen people make great breakthroughs when they start with daily acts of kindness and consistently show respect for everyone around them. Then it becomes easier to work up to acts of larger service. I have a wonderful friend named Shaloma who insists that everything she has to say to anyone can be said nicely. This doesn't make her a pushover. It just means that she works to cultivate the habits of speech that will allow her to communicate with everyone with respect and kindness. I cannot think of anyone who gives more to others or is more aware of the need for service.

The first thing to understand about service and giving is that we cannot and should not wait to give until we have more to give. We do not have to be rich to give. We do not have to be comfortable to give. There is not a better moment to give than in the present. We all have resources to share, even when we have few resources. We all have talents to share, time to share, and respect and compassion to share with others – gifts that come with no price tag. Smiling at someone who may not usually be seen or recognized offers a gift of respect. Noticing the people around you and being aware of their needs is an act of service and a gift to God.

Treating everyone in ways that honors their inherent dignity is a powerful gift to give the world. A homeless gentleman I often speak to asked me for something to eat, and when I gave him money, he explained that he wouldn't be allowed into any place in order to buy the food. I invited him to join me in a restaurant and together we shared a meal. Use your intuition about what is right in the moment and act for God out of the best self you can be and you will experience joy.

I worked in a maximum security prison while I was in law school. I worked as nurse and was assigned to care for a man who was on death row. I was afraid of the assignment and I prayed that the Lord would not let the man see my fear. I prayed that I would be able to set my fear aside and treat this inmate with respect and regard. I realized I might be the only person this man interacted with who might bring him a connection to God. I asked for God's help to accomplish this service. I addressed the man with respect and called him Mr. and I always inquired about how he felt. It was a challenge for me, but I learned a great deal from the experience and hoped that I had been of use to God in that cell.

When I feel unable to be kind in a situation, I try to quickly pray to let go of judgment and to send kind thoughts to the person I am having difficulty with. It is hard to do, and I often fail at being kind and nonjudgmental, but I am finding it a bit easier over time. When we really serve others, we are free of judgment and we expect nothing in return. That pure kind of service allows us not to feel attached to the outcome and frees us to act for God while leaving the outcome to God.

As a lawyer, I once represented a girl who was charged with the kind of felonies that could put her in jail for a very long time. I thought that I could serve her by giving her a feeling for a better life, and so I took her to a nice place to eat as a way of encouraging her. I also tried to help her in other ways because I had a false sense that it was in my power to do something that would immediately turn her life around. She showed absolutely no gratitude to me for what I was doing for her, and this made me very upset. Then I heard a voice say, *Will you continue anyway?* I realized that my ego was involved, and that I wanted to see immediate improvement in her. I expected her to show gratitude to me. My act of service was really just about me and my needs. I wanted to be seen as someone who was helping her in extraordinary ways.

Will you continue anyway? It was a question that helped me understood that my job was to follow the impulse to serve her and leave the rest to God. From then on, I did my best with her and gave the rest up to God, removing my ego from the situation and praying that she would feel God's presence in her life. I finally understood that the impact I could have in the world might not be something I would see or be recognized for, or even know about myself, and that really serving was what counted most.

Serving can be very difficult, but if we persevere, we can have an impact in ways we never even know. We can stand in the gap for someone else and feel compassion for them. We can attend to the person standing right next to us on the small scale, and also do what we can to address the huge problems that face the world. What can we do about a genocide going on in the world where hundreds of thousands have died and millions are displaced? Is it too large a problem to even think about? If we act for God, we know that raising awareness, raising money, and praying and offering our deep compassion and concern can make a difference – one person at a time and in ways that roll up into a large collective effort. We have the power to serve, and it can make an enormous difference in our local communities and in the global community.

Imagine the impact if each of us pledged to God that we would leave this world a better place than we found it. Make your life count by engaging in the kind of service that calls out to you. You might do something deliberately and continuously year after year, work on one project at a time, or participate in service with a burst of energy that accomplishes something specific within a certain period of time. There is no right or wrong way to serve, there is only the right way for *you* to serve, by contributing your particular gifts. Each of our contributions is valuable and each is appreciated by our Creator.

I have come to believe that when we offer monetary service by giving what we can, and spiritual service by doing what we can, we offer ourselves sacrificially to God. This doesn't mean giving with complaint and acting the part of the martyr, but instead, really giving freely from the level of soul.

When I hear a minister ask me to give to the level of "sacrifice," I now understand that this isn't about just putting more money in the offering plate until I have maximized what I can possibly give. When we give as a healthy and open sacrifice we *sanctify* our giving and make it holy.

The blessings we will receive when we turn our lives over to God and serve are enormous and never-ending. Serve well and put yourself on the line for the Divine. Give your service from the purest part of you, expecting nothing in return, and do everything you can to be of practical use to God.

Catherine Madera had a breakthrough that allowed her to find one way she could serve when she invited God to lead her to the right next step.

There were no extra cars in the driveway when I pulled up to the house that Monday night. "Guess I'm the only one to make it to Bible study," I thought. Truthfully, I considered skipping out too. It had been a long day and I was tired. But Sandy, the women's study leader, had already seen me pull up and had opened the front door to met me with a cheerful smile. She was full of enthusiasm and the aroma of freshly brewed coffee filled the air. "Come on in Catherine. I'm so glad you came!"

I admired Sandy. She was one of those women who seemed like she was living her life exactly like God wanted her to, wisely using her talents and gifts to serve him. As we sat down and opened our Bibles, I felt a familiar urgency rise up within me. *I want to serve God too!* But how could I? I'd walked with the Lord for a lot of years and seen Him work miracles in my life. I loved God, but had not yet found my place in ministry. There were so many things I was not good at; no musical talent, a mediocre cook, not a natural with children, and definitely not outgoing enough to reach out to people I didn't know. My weaknesses seemed so glaring. Didn't God have something for me to do?

As the Bible study wound down, I found the nerve to talk to Sandy about the question of my calling. After all, there was no one else there to make me feel self-conscious. "I feel like I want to serve God," I shared with Sandy. "I just don't know where, or how. Will you pray for me?"

"Of course!" Sandy smiled. "I'm excited for you. It is going to be great to see where God leads you now."

We prayed and said our goodbyes. All the way home, I thought about what she had said. She seemed so sure that God would find a place for me. What could it be? During the two weeks that followed, I didn't think about the question very much. Then at church, I noticed a sign-up sheet for a prayer chain that was forming. That was something even I could do. When the list of prayer chain volunteers was passed around, I took note of the name written after mine. I was supposed to call a woman I didn't know. When I called her with a request someone had made for prayer, we introduced ourselves over the phone. She told me she was a volunteer at a local pregnancy center and I found myself sharing an experience I had with an unplanned pregnancy earlier in my life. "With your experience, you could volunteer at the center, Catherine. May I give your name to my supervisor?" I hesitated only a moment before I agreed. Was this God, or only a coincidence?

Things happened very fast after that. The supervisor called me the next day and informed me of an upcoming volunteer training. It began the following week and I signed up, even with the doubts that had risen in my mind. I didn't think I was ready. I didn't know my Bible well enough. I wasn't outgoing. Besides, how could I know for sure that God was leading me in this direction?

The training was intense, and as it progressed, I felt afraid of the responsibility. As I studied the materials one day, I made up my mind to call the center and get out of my commitment. I would tell them that this just wasn't a good time for me. I would tell them that maybe next year would be better. At that moment, God spoke to my heart. *Read Gideon.* Gideon? Oh yeah, something about a fleece. I remembered the story vaguely from childhood. It took me some time to find the chapter in Judges, an old testament book I rarely looked up. *And the angel of the Lord appeared to him, and said to him, The Lord is with you, you mighty man of valor!*

I felt like laughing out loud. God was speaking to me that way too, a woman who had all the fears and inadequacies of Gideon. Reading on, I connected with the nature of God and understood that He didn't punish Gideon for being fearful. God even gave Gideon signs and wonders to prove He would be faithful. The story made it clear to me that God wanted to use me, if I was willing. He would prove Himself strong if I stepped forward.

There was no fleece for me to put out, but I began to look for signs that God wanted me to proceed in this ministry. There were many – a verse given to me unexpectedly at church; an e-mail from a friend. The greatest signs came from the time I spent in service. God gave me the strength I needed each day and I loved it. I enjoyed meeting with women, counseling them, and sharing my own experience. I even found I could be evangelistic, in my own way. "Can I pray for you?" Not long after I began volunteering, I gathered up the courage to reach out to one of our clients and make this offer to pray for her. She had experienced many hardships in her life and did not know the Lord. I was unsure how she would respond, but she said yes. After I prayed, I looked up and saw that tears had formed in her eyes. She wiped at them. "Thank you," she said simply.

A month after I started working at the center, I was evaluated by one of the supervisors. "You're a natural at this, Catherine." she told me, and gave me a supportive smile. Later on, I thought about being a modern-day Gideon – fearful, inadequate, and imperfect. But with God, I am a natural and I felt like a "mighty woman of valor."

I love a prayer that says, "I'm showing up for you today, Lord. Command my hands and feet. Command my talents and gifts. Command my resources, and let everything I am and can be in the future serve You."

We come into the world to live completely, to serve our brothers and sisters, and to be of use to God. The need for service is imprinted in the very DNA of our bodies and spirits. We offer our best service when we give it with generosity and love. When we live with everyday grace, we come into the fullness of God's plan for our life. Service brings light to the dark, gives hope to the hopeless, and brings miracles into the lives of those we touch and into our lives as well. May your service glorify your Creator and bring you joy.

Small Miracles

: Chapter Sixteen

IT TAKES A GREAT DEAL OF MOMENTUM TO CHANGE – it takes determination, patience, and, mostly, it takes faith that we can begin again in the present. For me, forgiveness and redemption are at the heart of transformation. We have to know how to accept responsibility for our actions and also to forgive ourselves and others. Then, we can redeem our lives and begin again, and this is nothing short of a miracle.

On this night, I was particularly aware of the high stakes we face as we make decisions about our lives. I showed my identification at the bullet-proof glass window and the corrections officer buzzed me through the locked doors. I passed through a waiting area where a few inmates milled around, waiting to see their families or to speak with a counselor. At a dark booth, I handed the guard the list of attendees who would be joining my course. As usual, the women who are part of this group were not ready for my visit. Since our time together was so limited, I wanted the women to be assembled in our meeting room and ready to get to work when I arrived at the Dade County Women's Annex. But in this environment where security is the top priority, it never seemed to happen like that.

I've been working with "Women Behind Bars" for some time now. I'm not sure how this part of my career evolved, I just felt called to do it as an extension of my work as a motivational speaker and life coach. I work with many successful women who are executives and leaders in their communities world-wide, and it just made sense to also work with groups of women whose life experiences and personal choices have been very different. As dissimilar as these groups of women are, I realized that all of us still share things in common. All of us face challenges, we all are given a set of life circumstances to which we must respond, and we all make the daily small choices and the big decisions that alter the course of our lives.

The Challenge to Change

What I see in every group I work with is the need for each of us to accept responsibility for our actions, face the truth about ourselves, learn new skills, become more resilient, move beyond being a victim, and set goals and achieve them with consistency and determination. Women in prison and women who live in freedom need the same skills and the same faith that change is possible. We all need the small miracles that can transform our lives.

I called the class to order quickly because we could not afford to waste time. I began this work with the hope that every woman in the facility would jump at any opportunity for growth and development. Some do, but the truth is that most don't. When I found myself judging the women for their lack of interest, I realized that I have often sabotaged myself in similar ways. Have you let opportunities pass? Have you always stepped up to the challenge to change? I think the truth is that, until our situation becomes unbearable, most of us drag our feet and avoid change when can. This realization helped me see that the women who are in jail are no different from the rest of us. Change comes hard to all of us.

The class began, and it was clear that some women wanted to be there and others were just using it as an excuse to leave their cells. Some hoped their participation would result in me putting in a good word with a judge. But others were there because they *did* want to change and at some level were willing to learn new things. My goal was to help them change their thinking patterns and their behavior. I understood from my work as a lawyer that it would take a tremendous shift to ensure that they didn't return to the system. If these women could really change, then it would be likely that their children and grandchildren would not end up in jail. If these women changed, the cycle of crime would end. Before each class I prayed a simple prayer, *Lord, please let them get it. Please let one person experience a breakthrough today.*

I didn't ask the women about the crimes for which they have been charged. The truth is elastic in jail, and I didn't want to engage in the stories of the past or with their patterns of manipulation. I tried to follow the principle set out by Christ, *Let she who is without sin cast the first stone.* We began with the understanding that all of us have made mistakes. Our task would be to privately accept responsibility for our actions and to work hard in our sessions together to change in the *now.* I worked to reinforce the truth that if they were able to change at a fundamental level, they might never have to come back to jail. I stressed the point that each of them could truly experience a rebirth into a new life.

Some of the women had played games so long that they approached this as just one more hustle. But as the weeks went by, their defenses fell and many of them admitted they had no idea what it would take to change. That was when the real work began. For some, this incarceration would be the final stop before a life sentence. Women in this situation would only be able to change what happened to them at the level of heart and soul, because they would probably not experience physical freedom on the outside ever again. For other women, this time in jail might serve as a wake-up call and an opportunity to change the course of the rest of their lives.

God Will Lead

Over the weeks of the course these women and I did our hard work together and I asked God to guide the process. It was deeply sad much of the time because it was clear that most of the women wouldn't make it. They had shut God out so firmly that they had locked themselves in a prison stronger that the walls that surround them here. But a few of the women did soften enough to let God lead the change in their lives, and seeing this happen was my joy.

Since that first group completed the course, I have seen many lives changed for the better. I have seen small miracles happen that have taken root and flourished into permanent change that has held for the long-term. Every time I begin the course, I look at the women in the room and ask God to provide a sense of grace that can touch each heart just for a moment. I ask that every one of these women feel the love of the Divine that this experience provide the spark a sense of self worth inside them that can grow to a sense of full and healthy empowerment. I asked for daily miracles to attend each of the women.

Step-by-step

What has allowed you to successfully change? Did you reach a point where it was more painful not to change than to face the need to change? Did you experience a spiritual breakthrough that fueled your change? I find that if I try to change something all at once, it does not work as successfully as when I take on change a small step at a time. When I can succeed at something small and then move forward to another small change, I can focus and succeed. When the change feels too daunting from the beginning, and if I don't experience some sort of breakthrough relatively soon, I tend to give up and walk way from the challenge. When I walk toward the change step-by-step, I tend to arrive at my destination.

Think back to a time when you successfully implemented a change and stuck to it in the long-term. Savor what that meant to you at the time and celebrate it again now. Then look at where you are with honesty and humility. What would you like to change about yourself and your life now? Take some time to make a list and then break down every change into its smallest parts. What can you reasonably take on today, this week, and this month that will provide the small breakthroughs that will give you momentum to make larger changes?

I invite you to ask God to be a part of your change. Ask Him to support your transformation with small miracles. Then, do you best, let go, and let God bring you the change you need – or something even better than what you can currently imagine. *Let go to grow* is an important theme in my work. This doesn't provide an excuse for not doing, procrastinating, or being lazy. It simply reinforces the need to do your best. God will step in to support your growth. Take the small steps to get the change underway and make note of the ways in which God provides small miracles. You'll be amazed at how often you experience that loving support.

Whether we live on the inside or outside of the prison system, we can be imprisoned in our minds. If we are held captive by our bad habits and our old and limiting thoughts, we can be caged by a lack of belief in ourselves and in God. Let's choose freedom and let God show us the way. I recently worked with a woman serving a sentence for her sixth DUI conviction. She was a doctor on the outside and had graduated at the top of her class. She received the highest score on the medical boards the year she took them. And then she became an inmate with a number, wearing prison blue, and having to face her demons head-on in prison. I pray that she will be willing to change and that she can be reborn as the healer God wants her to be. The key to her success will be her willingness to change. If she commits to her own transformation, God and people around her will help provide the keys to help her unlock the healthy potential for her life.

Some people change and others don't. The night I met Estella Washington, I worried that she would not change. I was discouraged and had begun to wonder if I could make a difference with the Women Behind Bars program. My experience as a criminal defense attorney meant that I didn't fear women like Estella, women charged with serious crimes, but it was hard to see the revolving door of women leaving prison only to return shortly thereafter. Estella was defiant in class and she was not happy with me at all. She was upset that I was not there to find her a job on the outside, so after the class I asked her to stay behind to talk. We had an honest and blunt discussion and I guess she must have decided that she could use some help at a deeper level before she focused on finding a job. She wasn't doing that well on her own and I was asking her to face up to that and make some significant changes in how she thought about herself and her life.

Estella became one of my best attendees. She expressed herself well as a poet and eventually would read her work in front of a large audience. But before she was successful in changing her life, she slipped yet again, and was rearrested about six months after her release. It was a challenge for her to accept responsibly for what she had done, but she did get her life back on track eventually. She ended up traveling a long way to get where she is today, and she learned important lessons about letting go and surrendering to God and not letting go of her potential.

Around three years ago, my whole life just fell apart. I had chosen to be with the wrong people and in a bad relationship and because of my poor decisions and my actions, I was arrested. I lost everything I had, my home and my car, and almost lost my mind. Through it all, I learned I could stand on the word of God. And I did, while I survived the fights on the inside and the pressures of incarceration. I knew I had to be strong in jail and that without the ability to post bail it would be a while before I was released. I felt alone, weary, and worried about my kids out there alone. Some nights, I just wanted to give up and end it all, and then I would realize that my kids would have nothing then. I came home with nowhere to go and nothing but the word of God. Me and my four small children stayed in a shelter for nine months and hung on.

I tried to start over, but before I could get things together, I was arrested again. My insides were all torn up with disgust at myself. I couldn't look anyone in the face. I felt trapped again, with my back against the wall and with no one to blame but myself. I was ashamed to face the people who had tried to help me, and I fell on my knees and said, "God, please change me from this animal that I am, and forgive me. Help me hold on and don't let go of me." I had to trust that God could do more for me than I had been able to do for myself. The program Women Behind Bars showed me how I could deal with my problems and how I could take my life up to another level.

I needed someone to guide me and give me the faith that all would be well. Ms. Lorna Owens was there by my side through thick and thin. When I got out, I went to school full-time, I went to church, and I became a responsible mother. Thanks to God! Because without his mercy and grace, I really don't know where I would be right now.

No matter what happens to me, I understand that I can throw up my hands in the air and ask God to give me strength. I believe he will! I know He will! I graduated from college and am working to be successful in my career. My children are doing fine now and all of us are back to living the reality of a good and Godly life. We have a nice four-bedroom town home and our future is going to be even better. I know we all have to go through our own struggles and tests, but I can tell you that sharing your testimony with someone who is going through a similar situation will inspire them not to give up. Let someone know that help is on the way.

I understand that I had to first know in my heart that I wanted a better life and that I deserved a better life. I needed help from people to learn how to get a new life going. But, I was the only one who knew what needed to be done and how it must be done, and it was up to me to make the decision to change. Now I can offer advice to women who are in a similar situation. I tell them the road may be long and the streets may be dark, but there is light at the end of the tunnel, if you allow your faith to carry you to your destiny. I have a changed and renewed mind and spirit. I had to go through everything I went through to get what my God had waiting for me. Although I had blamed others for what had happened to me, I finally understood that I was the only one who really had control over my life.

I asked for the small miracle of not letting go of my potential. I also needed the miracle of trusting God. Before the Women Behind Bars program, I didn't know a stranger could care about me. There was something healing about realizing I was valued, and that someone thought I had potential. When God is for you, who could be against you?

Just What We Need

I believe that people who have been incarcerated can change, and that any and all of us can experience a true metamorphosis. We can stop being who we were, and become the person we were meant to be – a person with new skills, compassion, and the ability to treat ourselves and others with the same respect God shows us. For the women in my program, even a small shift in consciousness is a miracle. We celebrate their graduation from the program as the new birth it is. We have a party and share a lovely cake, as if celebrating a birthday. From that day forward, the women who have gone through the program have the power to make different choices, and they have the faith to ask God for what they need. We laugh, we joke, we sing, and when we fall we start all over again, because every day provides a new chance to choose to live in grace.

Sometimes, the miracle that comes is not a life-altering experience. It can arrive as a beautiful and simple blessing. Peggy Frezon experienced a small miracle that reminded her that she could receive just what she needed on any given day.

I couldn't drive my car in heavy rain because the windshield wipers hadn't worked in months. The wiper motor sounded like it was trying to go; it hummed and groaned. But the wipers jerked up only a fraction of an inch and flopped down again. My husband wasn't good at car repairs and we didn't have enough money yet to get the wipers fixed. I just drove the car on sunny days and hoped for good weather.

One day, I had to get to the pharmacy, there was no choice. It was getting dark and overcast. If I was going to get there and back before the rain hit, I had to act fast. I jumped into the car and just as I started off, a light sprinkle began. As I finished my errand and returned to the car, the rain was coming down in torrents. It looked like the rain would be falling for a long time. I didn't think I could wait it out. I prayed, "Okay, God. Please either stop this rain, or make my wipers work. Please help me get me home safely." I held my breath and pulled the wiper lever.

The wipers didn't budge and I heard the sound of the failing motor groaning. I wondered if I could move the wipers manually. If I stopped, got out and pushed the wipers by hand and did this every few yards, could I make it home? I didn't want to do anything dangerous. I drove very slowly, struggling to see past the sheet of rain drowning the windshield. Just as I was getting ready to pull over and manually wipe my windows, the far wiper swept over in the most unexpected and unnatural movement, clearing the rain away from the windshield! Just one motion, and then it stopped. I couldn't believe it!

I drove a little farther, carefully, and then, just as the rain was building up again, swoosh! Every time the rain began to obstruct my view, that wiper cleaned my window. I got home without a problem. I wondered why God hadn't made my wipers work the regular way, or even fixed them for good. But then I realized how amazing God was. He gave me enough to get home. My husband and I would need to see to the necessary repair as soon as we had the money, but I had received the blessing of just what I needed – not more than I needed, and nothing less.

We Can Always Go Home

I THINK OF GOD AS MY HOME, and so no matter what, I know I can always return home to my connection with my Father. Remember the story of the prodigal son and how welcoming and forgiving his father was? We will always be forgiven and we will always be loved by God.

Susan Karas shares a story about her father that can also serve as a reminder of how our Father in Heaven works in our lives as well.

Sunlight glinted off the blaring trumpets of the marching band. I burrowed into my jacket to ward off the autumn chill, breathing in the sharp tang of dried leaves. Festive floats lumbered by, followed by baton twirlers. Finally, marching in proud rows, came the veterans we'd come to honor.

I missed the connection with my dad more than ever. He was a vet from World War II. As a young girl, I'd nestle by his side and listen to tales of his service overseas. Sometimes, he'd dig out his cigar box and show me photos of his army buddies and the medals he'd been awarded. As I held them in my small hands, I couldn't help thinking there wasn't anything my dad couldn't do.

Standing in the crowd watching the parade, it hit me again that dad couldn't do many things anymore. He couldn't march in a parade. He'd recently suffered a stroke and was moving much slower. His thinking was often muddled. But worst of all, speaking had become difficult for him, which all but ended our phone conversations. With he and my mother in Kentucky and me living in New York, that was how we'd done most of our connecting. I missed talking with him so much.

As soon as I got home, I grabbed the phone and punched in his number. I just had to talk to him, even if he could only listen.

"Hi, mom, can you put dad on?"

"You know, he's embarrassed to talk on the phone, Sue."

"I know," my voiced cracked. "But please, just get him?"

She hesitated, but called, "It's for you, Jim."

"H'lo."

"Hi dad, happy Veteran's Day.

"Who…. cahh…wing…? My stomach somersaulted at his garbled speech. It was worse than last time.

"It's me, Sue." I fought back tears.

I wanted my other dad back, the one who sat talking with me for hours. The dad who wrapped me in warm bear hugs, the one who could always make me believe everything would be all right, no matter the problem I brought him. Memories of the dad who was always there for me raced through my mind as I scrambled for words. "Dad," I took a steadying breath. I wanted to say so much, to tell him how much he meant to me, how much I missed him. Instead I said something I hadn't said in a long time.

"I love you, dad." There was a long pause, "Dad?"

"You…uu…uuu…" He struggled to speak. I could hear his frustration. "G'bye." I heard a click, then the dial tone. I hung up the phone feeling empty.

Shortly after that call, my dad passed away. I never had the chance to talk to him again. At the funeral, I stared at his pictures trying to connect. It seemed impossible that he was gone. I was glad I had told him I loved him. But I wondered, had he really understood?

When I got back to New York, I sat on my bed and opened the lid of the cigar box I'd loved as a girl. Mom had wanted me to have it and I gently held dad's medals and photos. How I wish he had been able to talk to me on Veteran's Day. The room seemed stifling it seemed that nothing would ever be right again, not without dad to make me believe things would work out. *God, please give me a sign. Did he know how much I loved him?*

Some time later, I found myself driving aimlessly and finally stopped when my stomach growled with hunger. I pulled into a fast food restaurant, placed my order, and stood at the counter lost in thought.

"Excuse me there, sweetie." An older man reached past me to get some napkins.

"What? Oh, sorry." I drew in a sharp breath, he looked so much like my dad with the same white hair and the same silver-rimmed glasses. He even moved like my dad. I stepped back to get out of his way, and to my horror, started weeping. Sweetie? That's what dad always called me. I lowered my head and shaded my eyes as tears coursed down my cheeks.

The nice old fellow must have moved beside me because I felt a comforting hand on my shoulder. Then I felt a gentle pat on my back. A sweet peace settled over me. *Everything will be all right,* I seemed to hear. I turned to thank the kind stranger but he wasn't there! How was that possible? I had felt his warm touch on my back. I looked around and spotted a white-haired gentleman at a booth in the far corner, eating a burger. He couldn't have been comforting me *here,* if he was way over *there* enjoying his lunch.

I stared out the front window for a moment to collect my thoughts. The sunlight glinted off a flag pole, with the red, white and blue flying proudly in the breeze. Suddenly I knew that dad had heard what I had said on Veteran's Day but couldn't respond. I felt the presence of an angel reassuring me that everything was going to be all right. I was in awe, just like when I was a little girl there *was* nothing my dad couldn't do. There was nothing God couldn't do.

Finding Comfort

Sometimes *going home* means not going home to a literal physical place, but returning to a place in your mind or heart where you feel safe and comforted. Since we really are children of God, it makes sense to tune into that reality and make the most of the connection with the Divine. Dallas Nicole Woodburn remembers a childhood that kept her grounded in the love and encouragement she received from her mother.

I took my first steps holding a large plastic ball. It was painted with a picture of Grover from Sesame Street, my favorite television character. We called it my "magic Grover ball" because I thought that when I held it in my arms I could walk. I wouldn't even try to walk without it. Then one day, the unthinkable happened. My magic Grover ball popped. What would I do without my invisible safety net? I would never walk again. I was doomed to a lifetime of rug-burned knees from crawling quickly over carpeted floors.

Then my mother stepped in and, after drying my tears, she positioned herself across the room. It must have seemed like she was miles away. She spread her arms wide. "Dallas," she coaxed. "Come here. Come to mommy."

I stood on my wobbly little legs, not believing that my magic Grover ball was really gone. Didn't Mommy see that? Didn't she realize there was no way I could walk to her without it? "Come on, Dallas. Walk to Mommy." My mother says I looked her square in the eyes and took a few hesitant steps. Those steps turned into a few more confident steps, these turned into walking all the way across the room–*without* the mystical powers of my magic Grover ball! I was walking with encouragement from my mom.

My mother and I went on almost-daily walks around the neighborhood, and as I learned to walk better, I climbed out of my stroller and walked beside her, holding her hand. Even though I was very young, I still have memories of these walks. I remember being filled with a sense of comfort and peace. I remember gentle sunlight filtering through the leaves of the trees above us, the warm security of my mother's hand in mine, the sound of her voice as we sang songs together. Who could ask for anything more?

As I've grown older, things have changed and life is more hectic. I'm a college sophomore now, taking a full course-load, volunteering as a tutor for grade-school kids, and working as a freelance writer. My mother is the head of a department at work and runs marathons and, of course, keeps the household running smoothly. But, no matter how busy we get, over the years one aspect of our lives has remained wonderfully the same – our shared walks.

In high school, when I still lived at home, Mom and I took our dog for a stroll around the neighborhood nearly every evening. We talked, we laughed, we bonded, and I felt her love as encouragement to live a fulfilled life. Although I'm now away at college, I live close enough to visit every few weekends. I always look forward to taking a walk with my mom. As we walk the neighborhood, it's as if nothing has changed. I know when I have something to say my mom will listen. If I have a problem, she will help me figure out a way to fix it.

Mom and I have struggled through our share of problems together. I was born prematurely and weighed just a couple of pounds. Back in 1987, the chances that I would survive were extremely small. My mother was stricken with preeclampsia, a terrifying condition that threatened her life as well as mine. A team of medical professionals kept us alive, and now all these years later, we still both enjoy robust health. I thank God for the love he shows us and I thank Him for my walks with Mom. Our ritual of walking together has helped us have a powerful bond.

Together, we have hiked up to the summit of Mt. Whitney and down to the bottom of the Grand Canyon. We have walked through shopping malls searching for the perfect dress for my prom, and when I walked across the stage and received my high school diploma I knew my mother walked with me. Together, we walked the grounds of college campuses searching for the college of my dreams, and I know my mom will always be there cheering me on as I step across the threshold and into my future.

Looking back, I realize that my special first steps weren't because of my "magic Grover ball" after all. The real magic came from my mother's love and encouragement. Together and with God, we'll walk along life's winding paths, and when I have a little wobbly-legged toddler of my own one day I'll know just what to do. "Come on," I'll say. "Let's go for a walk."

A Bounteous Home

Every Christmas, I return to Jamaica to spend the holidays in a place that feels like my true home. When I arrive through Montego Bay, I often experience a particularly exciting homecoming. In the lobby of the airport, travelers are often greeted with the music of a mento band and women who sing Jamaican folk songs. The women are dressed in stunning layered skirts, white blouses with ruffles, and wear red-striped bandanas on their heads – an impressive and beautiful head-dress. This is the national dress of Jamaica. As they sing, I am always moved to tears, overwhelmed with the emotion of coming home. I look at the women with their wide hips, round faces, broad noses and beautiful smiles and I celebrate the power of these beautiful Jamaican women.

My experience of my homeland and of our family home was always that of being surrounded by love. Our family was poor, but we felt like we had plenty. We grew our own fruits and vegetables and our family relied on the Lord. Now, as I drive home to Mandeville on my return trips, I pass through the lovely small towns of Spanish Town, May Pen, and Porus. These towns are filled with the bustle of markets and colorful street vendors offering roasted yams, peanuts, wood carvings, baskets, mango, pineapples, sour and sweet sop, and itahoti apple. To get to Mandeville, I drive high into the hills. I climb until I feel I could touch the sky. The higher I climb, the greener the vegetation becomes and every time I return home, I am filled with gratitude for the simple grandeur of the place.

When my mother hears the car coming, she comes to sit by the door to greet me. She is always glad to see me and has a wonderful Jamaican meal ready. The comfort of her love and care surround me.

Years ago, I made a promise to know the land of my birth better, and so on each visit I try a new experience. Recently, I rafted down the Martha Brae, the longest river in the parish of Trelawny on the north coast of the island. The river begins in the mountains and loops and winds its way to the Caribbean Sea. I made the trip on a bamboo raft through lush tropical forests guided by my rafts man. This trip gave me time to reflect on how beautiful the world is and how wonderful it is that God makes this earth such a bounteous home for his children. How welcome we can feel when we connect with God's love.

What I have learned from my own life experience, what I have learned from Women Behind Bars, and from the successful professional women who attend my workshops around the world, is that we have an authentic self to which we can always return home. I have also learned that our connection to God is a home to which we can always return as well.

With God's help, we can find the gifts we were meant to give the world and an abundant and blessed life can be ours. My prayers these days have become shorter and more frequent. I often pray, "God, I know that you are love and I promise to seek Your guidance in all I say and do." The essence of my relationship with God has become more immediate, truly intimate, and very simple.

No matter where you find yourself, return to God's love as often as you can. None of us is the sum of our mistakes. We are God's children and we can undertake life's journey knowing that we can begin again, we can do better, and we can keep forgiveness in our hearts. We can always go home. We may need to face tears and challenges in the process of going home. We may feel regret and shame, and we may miss what has been lost and grieve for what never came to pass. But, we will be blessed by returning to the spiritual home that is always near at hand. I encourage you to find some silence, pray, and let yourself return home today.

Gratitude

WE SET THE TONE OF OUR DAYS with what we think about, what we fixate on, and how we choose to read our experiences. Are we optimistic or pessimistic, complaining or grateful? "Give God the praise. Give God the praise!" the minister shouted out from the front of the church. And all of us who had gathered in that little room would respond, "Praise God." That was how things went in the church in which I was raised. I heard "Hallelujah!" being shouted out in joy before I had a clue what hallelujah meant. Now I know it is the highest praise I can give God, and that doing so celebrates all the blessings I have, and helps call in the new blessings I seek.

During the darkest times of my life, I struggled to put fires out and to deal with stress and my attitude declined. I did not give thanks for a time and I felt there was nothing in my life to be thankful for. During the process of sinking low, I learned I still had a great deal to be thankful for and I learned to be appropriately grateful. Now, I feel I need to offer my praise and thanks in double in order to make up for the years when I was ungrateful.

Give Thanks And Praise

On your best days and your worst days, make sure God knows you give thanks and praise. I believe we can praise and pray our way out of the most difficult situations in our lives. We can praise like a prize fighter in the fight for our lives. We can praise when all we see is a little sliver of light shining through the darkness. Make your escape from trouble with praise. Praise even when the news from the doctor is not good, when one more bank has turned down the loan for your new business. Praise God even when tragedy strikes, because without the dark we cannot appreciate the light. Without pain, we don't know the absence of pain. There is always some good to be taken from even the worst of times, and when life is going along well, we should find it easy to stay grateful.

What if, by focusing on what we are grateful for, we could be met with a feeling of peace, even in the little cranky moments of our lives? Nancy Lucas has found a way to invite more kindness into her work as a waitress. What she calls her "three percent perspective" helps her feel more connected to God at work, and perhaps it also allows her to attend to people with the grace of an angel, giving them a taste of peace as well.

It was a beautiful night and I served an open-air table of four people who gazed at the stars and enjoyed the fresh ocean breeze. The evening went very well and I worked hard to serve them in the best sense of that word. Their fresh seafood platters were excellent and arrived at just the right time, and we enjoyed a jolly time bantering back and forth. Their bill was $120 and they ask to split it. One man gave me a $100 bill and asked for $30 in change, another man gave me a credit card and asked me to charge $70 on it. After the party left the restaurant, I found they had left only $2 cash on the table and had added $2 to the credit card total for my tip. In my fatigue at the end of a long shift, I was dumbfounded as to why they would leave only a $4 tip–that is only three percent!

"What did I do wrong?" I asked my co-workers, showing them the receipt. They chimed in with "that sucks" and other negative statements about my customers. I joined in saying nasty things, but I immediately knew that my attitude was wrong. I have learned that whatever I do, I need to work at it with all my heart. My work reflects who I am, not other people, and I want to set my own standards for how I live. I am working for myself and the Lord, and I had broken a pledge I had made to myself when I took this job – that I would be very grateful for the work and my ability to do the work.

I had been injured for a time with severe carpal tunnel syndrome that made it painful to use my wrists and hands, and during the last few months of my pregnancy with my daughter, I had been so ill that I could not drive, exercise, or walk very far. At the end of the pregnancy, I couldn't even sit up for more than a few minutes. My husband and I had gone for three years without a steady second income, and it had made us feel poor and stressed. When I felt well again, I had promised myself that I would be appreciative of feeling healthy enough to work. I had vowed to trust God and to give thanks for my many blessings every day.

Most of my fellow service workers are in the habit of looking immediately at the check and they grumble if they receive anything less than a twenty percent tip. They also complain when an older couple, a group of college students, or someone who seems like a foreigner is seated in their section, assuming a low tip will result. I try not to bring that kind of negativity to work, because I want to live with peace and gratitude and show the Lord what I can do. I try to serve people with an open heart, and every night I end up going home with a proportionately greater amount of tip money.

This night, I had given in to feeling terrible about my customers and the small tip. If you are quicker at math than I am, you will have noticed that I had made a mistake. My customers had given me $140 total, which left a $20 tip plus the additional four they had added at the end. Because I didn't receive the tip in the way I expected, I assumed the worst. Their "measly" $4 tip was instead a generous tip of exactly twenty percent.

I wonder if we sometimes miss gifts we are given because they come in a form that is different from what we expect. I went back to correct the perception my co-workers had of my customers, and I prayed and sent my customers loving kindness, to make up for the harsh words I had said behind their backs. It is a lesson I think of often.

Gratitude Is A State of Mind

We can stay centered and maintain an attitude of gratitude in situations where things seem to be within our control, but what can we do when the list of things that goes wrong seems insurmountable? For whatever reason, there are times in our lives when things go wrong in multiple ways. Looking back, we see these very challenging times as a blessing, but when we're in the midst of the mess, it can feel like just too much. Dahlia Walker saw a year that held a great deal of promise turn into the worst year of her life.

I immigrated to the United States from Jamaica in 1979 with my parents. All my life, I lived with my parents and in 1979, as we immigrated, the parent-child dynamic changed. At eighteen years of age, I became the head of the household and instead of living with my parents, my parents lived with me. This shift worked well for all three of us and we shared mutual respect and were also great friends.

Time passed as we worked to build a life in Florida. I had been looking forward to 1997 with great expectation. This would be the year I achieved my goal. After nine and half years of going to college part-time, and then attending law school full-time I would finally realize my dream of graduating with a law degree. But, as 1996 drew to a close, I realized that 1997 was going to be unlike any other in my life for several reasons.

On the morning of December 31, 1996 my father died from lung cancer. He had smoked for fifty years and had quit a decade before, but this was not enough to stop the destruction of his body. He took the disease in stride and he never complained. We knew his time was short, but his death still hit me and my mother hard.

It doesn't matter if your loved one dies at age seven or seventy-five; the loss of someone you love deeply is always devastating. When my father died, I felt as if I had physically lost a part of my body. The emptiness was overwhelming. I was a law clerk with a criminal law firm in Coconut Grove, Florida, and I was at the Miami-Dade criminal Courthouse when I received the call that my father was gone. As my boss drove me back to the office to get my car, I felt as if I was floating in the sky and looking down at everyone going about their business as if nothing had happened. I wanted to scream out to people that they needed to stop, that my father was dead! How could people be driving around and laughing and talking at this moment? That's when I understood that no matter what, life goes on with or without us, and that this is a good thing.

We buried my father on January 4th and I returned to law school for my final semester a couple of days later. As hard as it was for me to deal with the loss of my father, I know it was even more difficult for my mother. Theirs was a love affair that spanned the decades. They were inseparable. Soon after my father died, I noticed that my mother's right arm was shaking. I thought it was probably her nerves and her reaction to dealing with Daddy's death. A week went by and the shaking did not go away, so I took her to the doctor. He referred her to a specialist and two weeks later another "1997" moment occurred when my mother was diagnosed with Parkinson's disease.

My mother was a tower of strength through her illness. She always had the right Jamaican saying to fit any occasion. She was funny, saucy, loving, and biting all at the same time. Together we took on the challenges of law school, her health, and our very tight finances. It had been difficult to quit my job to go to law school full-time. My parents had been receiving small social security checks each month, but with my father's passing his check stopped coming. I had received a Dean's Honor Scholarship from the University of Miami and my tuition was paid for the three years I attended law school, but I had to borrow heavily just to live. We lived in a modest townhouse and had tons of credit-card debt and no breathing room. My mother and I held out hope that we could make it until I graduated from Law School. Surely at that point I would have job offers up and down. We imagined me getting a good job and our life stabilizing soon after that.

On the way to the law school to hand in my final paper and my last exam, the air conditioning in my old car died on the Palmetto Expressway in Miami. In May in Miami, you only have to breathe to sweat. The humidity level makes being anywhere without air conditioning difficult. I had to push on without the slightest thought of fixing the air conditioning because I had no money at all. Mother was there again with her encouragement and her faith that God would help keep me cool.

My graduation was scheduled for Mother's Day, and my mother said that we could not let the occasion pass without celebrating. Finally, my dreams would be realized. From the time I was a child I wanted to be a lawyer and an advocate. Family and friends gathered with us to celebrate my graduation and I was filled with emotion. I was seeing my dream come true, but sadly my father was not there with us.

All lawyers have a right of passage to experience–the summer between graduation and taking the bar exam. Every day for two months, I trekked in my no-air-conditioning car from Miami Lakes to Coral Gables to study for the bar exam. Money was exceptionally tight, and each time I thought we were going to go hungry, the next day God answered our prayers and an angel sent us money. Prayer had become our way of coping with life. We survived because we read the Bible and said novenas to St. Jude daily. We prayed without ceasing and hoped to see the light. I was broke and couldn't work, because I had decided to devote full-time to studying for the bar exam. I thought this would ensure that I would pass and get a job as quickly as possible.

One day the cable bill was three months behind and the cable man showed up to disconnect our service. I had sent a payment, but it wasn't the full amount and the company had not yet recorded the payment I had sent. The cable man wanted a check for the full amount or he was going to disconnect our service. For us, cable wasn't a luxury. With my mother's Parkinson's disease, television was her only form of company while I was away studying. Cable television was my mother's lifeline to the world. I begged him not to disconnect our service, but he said he had no choice. He had to disconnect it from the box in the street.

I began praying like an evangelist. I called on God out loud and begged Him not to take the only form of relief my mother had. The cable was never disconnected. My brother Lloyd sent us money several times that summer, and somehow we were able to make it. One day, when we were down to our last few dollars, my mother's cousin in Jamaica sent us $400 out of the blue. What a blessing! If she had given us four million dollars it could not have meant more to us at the time.

The bar exams in Florida are held in Tampa towards the end of July.

The Saturday before the exam, the air conditioner at my townhouse exploded and burst into flames–another 1997 moment. We heard the explosion and couldn't figure out what it was until I saw flames billowing in the back of the house. I called 911 and ran to get a neighbor. The neighbor came to our rescue and put out the fire before the fire department arrived. We thanked everyone for their help, and when they left, the floodgates opened. I cried like I had never cried in my life. I felt as if I was going to loose my mind. I began to question God. My mother held me in her arms as I cried out like a person possessed. My mother soothed me like a young child. All of my thoughts and feelings poured out. I felt I was doing everything I was supposed to, and now I was at the end of the line and everything was falling apart around me. I had my law school diploma sitting in my drawer and wasn't life supposed to be getting better by now?

My mother assured me that things would get better, and encouraged me not to give up. We prayed and I calmed down. I got up the next morning with a renewed vigor and decided that I would rise above the summer of 1997 with God's help.

My mother did not want to be left behind in Miami when I went to take the bar exam. By this time the Parkinson's disease was taking a toll on her, especially at night. She had now abandoned her bedroom and was sleeping in my room. I had to take her with me to Tampa. When I arrived in Tampa to check in at the hotel, my credit card was declined. That was the one card that I had made payments on and I was counting on it to work. I said a silent prayer and tried another card, one that had no chance of working – it was accepted.

I took the two-day exam and my mother and I went to the Tampa airport to return to Fort Lauderdale. After we ate two hotdogs, I was left with 74 cents in my purse and had no idea where my next dollar would come from. A friend picked us up at the airport and learned how broke we were. He gave me $100 and offered to pay my mortgage for a couple of months until I could find a job. I will never forget that kindness. I learned that God always sends angels to help us.

The day after returning from the bar exam, I took my car, which by now was overheating and making awful noises as well as having no air-conditioning, and made the rounds of a number of employment agencies looking for a job as a secretary. I had bills to pay and an ailing mother to care for, so I had to do whatever I could until I received the notice that I had passed the bar.

I got a job as a legal secretary for an aircraft maintenance company in Miami, and that's when things started to look up. I met two wonderful attorneys at the company who respected me as a lawyer. I worked hard at everything they gave me, whether it was reviewing a contract, taking dictation, or typing a letter. Most importantly, I got a paycheck every week. I began paying our bills and the pressures started lifting. My car's engine needed an expensive repair that was not within my reach to afford. Another of God's angels, the owner of the repair shop, agreed to fix the car and let me pay him in installments.

By now, it was time to receive the results of the bar exam. I failed by a half a point. Half a point! I didn't even know a person could receive half a point for an answer. Devastation hit me again. I needed to pass this exam so I could find a job as a lawyer. What was going on in the cosmos? Surely this was some supernatural force working against me. I had studied hard for years, I had applied myself with every thing I had, and I had failed the bar exam. Forget the embarrassment of facing friends and family, the private humiliation alone was overwhelming.

The angels at my secretarial job stepped in and assured me that I could stay and work for them as long as I wanted. At this point, I had no choice because no one was going to hire me as a lawyer before I had passed the bar. I stayed at my job and worked overtime whenever I could and I gradually paid my bills. I was still driving my car without air conditioning but at least it ran, and I added teaching part-time at Miami Dade College to the mix and collected two modest paychecks.

By Thanksgiving of that most difficult year, my mother's ex-employer, who also owned a small storefront plaza, offered me a room for rent in order to open my own firm. The room was just a room with holes in the walls and dirty carpet, but I transformed that room into a workable office while I studied for the bar exam.

I look back on 1997 as the most turbulent year of my life. I lost my father, I failed the bar exam, no one offered me a job as a lawyer, I was penniless and nearly homeless, my mother was diagnosed with Parkinson's, and I was in debt up to my eyeballs. My mother died of colon cancer in 2000, but from the dark days of 1997 to her death, we took comfort in each other and felt blessed by our connection and our shared faith in God.

I learned a valuable lesson in that terrible time. I came to understand that no matter how much you plan, you are not in control. I learned to give my life to the Lord, and to trust Him to direct me. And most importantly, I learned that gratitude was a state of mind and that there was much to be thankful for, even in the midst of the crisis.

I went on to pass the bar on the second try, open my own law practice, and become the first female to head the Caribbean Bar Association. I was named as a Woman Inspiring Hope in 2004 by the Florida Association of Women Lawyers. I am a mediator, an arbitrator, and a special magistrate for the City of Miramar; a hearing officer for Broward County Animal Court; and the great gift of my life is that I am married to a wonderful man. I am deeply grateful for my life, for every part of my life, for the best and worst of times in my life.

The Richness of Life

Praising God and feeling gratitude help your wings of faith grow stronger. Faith supports you in soaring above the pain and the hurt in your life. Praise and gratitude sustain like nothing else can. With gratitude, you can feel some sense of peace, even when your heart is breaking.

Offer thanks to God for the minutes of every day, for the chance to do it all again, and even for the things that irritate and challenge you. Give thanks for the imperfection and richness of life.

I find that if I stay *praised up*, I do not worry about missed opportunities. God always answers in some way and a spirit of gratitude takes care of the details.

A spirit of gratitude overcomes self pity and gives me a feeling of sustaining grace. Karen Ward lives in Australia with her husband and three boys. At times her frazzled nerves make it hard for her to feel gratitude, but laughter and a light touch help her return to joy.

I turned the key in the ignition. Nothing happened. *Oh, Lord. Please let it start.* I tried again. Nothing happened. *No, Lord, please, not today. They've waited all week and they're so excited.* After four more tries, I had to admit to my three boys that we had a problem.
"But we're going to the zoo!"

"I know, baby, but the car won't start."

"Can't you fix it, Mummy? You said we were going to the zoo." Gasping through his sobs, Josh's earnest pleas tugged at my heart. I was power-less to do anything but hug him and resort to offering a favorite DVD while we waited for the mechanic to arrive.

The mobile mechanic tried everything he could think of before giving us the bad news. He managed to make the car drivable, but we had to take it straight to the auto electrician. I guess I should have been grate-ful that it wasn't a long drive. *But, Lord, please could you let them fix it quickly?*

"Are we going to walk to the zoo, Mummy?"

"No, these men are going to try and fix the car, then we can go to the zoo."

"And see the gorillas?"

"Yes, we'll see the gorillas." Joshua launched into his gorilla imperson-ation, and I walked the boys to the pet shop in the mall to distract them for a while.

"Puppies, Mummy! Can we get a puppy?"

"No, Matt. You know Daddy doesn't want a puppy yet. We're here to look at the animals, not buy them. Mikey Cat wouldn't like a puppy. Remember how we talked about that?" The sales assistant approached and Matt spoke up in a very clear voice, "When our cat dies we will get a puppy." I didn't bother trying to explain.

"Mummy, is it time to go to the zoo yet?"

"The car is still being fixed, remember? When the car gets fixed, we'll go to the zoo." And so the afternoon wore on and wore us down. At last, my mobile phone rang. The shop would have to keep the car until tomorrow.
"Boys, that was the man who has the car."
"Can we go to the zoo now?"

"Well, no, it looks like we'll have to go to the zoo next week."

Their little faces drooped so far I wasn't sure how I'd cope if my next distraction didn't work. "But, we get to catch a bus home!" I held my breath as they hesitated.

"Yey!" said one boy finally, and the other two followed.

I was looking forward to getting home, putting Ethan to bed and giving the big boys a snack outside so I could sit down with a cuppa, and call my husband Jason to tell him about the day. When we arrived at our stop, I wrestled the boys, the stroller, and the bags to the pavement. I reached for my house keys. They weren't in my pocket. I rifled in my handbag. No keys. I had a sinking feeling in the pit of my stomach. I had given the auto repairman *all* of my keys since I had assumed I'd be picking the car up today. We were locked out of the house. Ethan started to cry. I wanted to join him. Joshua rubbed his eyes and asked for the four hundredth time that day when we would go to the zoo.

"What's wrong, Mummy?" Matthew was perceptive and could tell I was about to lose it.

"Well, we need to call Daddy. Mummy has left her keys with the car."

By the time my husband pulled into the driveway, we were a total mess. Matthew had ordered a game of chasing Josh around the front yard. Josh had agreed, but only as long as he could be the gorilla, thumping and screaming at the top of his voice. Ethan had wanted to join in the game too, but as to be expected with a tired baby, he had soon tripped over, and all had come to tears.

That's how my husband found us. Me, completely overwhelmed but trying to take charge, Ethan, screaming as if he was in need of the emergency department; Matt roaring like a lion and chasing Joshua who was still a loud gorilla. Jason raised one eyebrow as he took this in and looked at me. "You couldn't go to the zoo, so you brought the zoo to us?"

The laughter in his eyes brought me relief, and I laughed too. I realized that this day was only twenty four hours long, just like all the others. God would get us through, again.

Gratitude Gives Back

Gratitude is not contingent on what we have or don't have. It is an expression of appreciation for everything in our lives – the sunshine and the rain. Today, I open my door I look out on the water. It is an exquisite shade of blue and it gleams. I say, "Thank you, God." And I walk around Miami Beach in awe of everything that surrounds me. I appreciate the simple pleasures of being able to walk to the post office and the supermarket. I appreciate my work and my rest; the opportunities to learn and share that come with traveling, and the pleasures of coming home.

When I am in Jamaica, I always attend the Word of Life Worship Center in Old Harbour, my brother's church. One especially memorable Christmas, the guest pastor, Rev. Steven Samuels, explained that there is incredible power in our words and that we need to proclaim our relationship with God to others. I became more vocal about my gratitude after that, and I always feel the power of the energy that comes when I say or write about how grateful I am. Gratitude seems to come back to me. I thank God for the water as I walk on the beach to-day, and the water seems to answer, "You're welcome."

Nicole Wild grew up in the bush in Australia. She survived poverty, child abuse, tough times of every sort, and struggled to finish high school. She seemed to have every reason to give up on life. But, Nicole had what she described as a passion for taking care of herself. She wanted to be self-sufficient more than anything, and when her mother died of cancer, Nicole understood that her drive to help herself survive and then thrive could be extended as a life mission to help others. She is a tremendous success now, but before she became fully empowered, she had to begin at the beginning.

I started working as a bus boy and then, once I had some grounding, I moved on to work at a bank. I worked so hard that I was able to move up into business banking. One day, my bank manager suggested I enter the Miss Australia Awards Program. Being from the bush and having so little education, this seemed to be an unreachable goal, but my participation in the pageant opened the door for me to do the nonprofit work that changed my life forever.

Because of the difficult experiences I had gone through, I was able to see the needs of others clearly. I understood from my own experience and from the experience of my mother that many women couldn't live up to their full potential because of family problems, societal issues, economic factors, health problems, and other obstacles.

I dove into fundraising for women's causes with my whole heart and was recognized for these efforts in the Miss Australia Awards Program. This experience, and the power of prayer, helped me step into the job of being executive director of The Women's Alliance in Miami. I believe that to empower women to become truly self-sufficient, they need to have the right tools and mentors. Women can move their lives from one chapter to the next, progressing from homelessness, poverty, and despair to achieving goals and becoming self-sufficient financially. In order to achieve this, they have to be able to project their inner power in ways people can see. They have to have the basic tools and support in order to make this miracle happen.

Our organization implemented a social enterprise model to create Chapter 2, a high-quality resale clothing store located in an economically challenged neighborhood. All proceeds from the sale of merchandise go to support The Women's Alliance mission so that low-income women have the clothes they need for job interviews and work. Chapter 2 also gives back to the community by providing transitional employment and internship programs. A training initiative provides inspiration and support to help women advance and keep them moving forward. People need to be provided with opportunities to help them build their résumés and ongoing support to help them learn how to create the lives they were meant to live.

The Women's alliance now has affiliates in forty cities across the United States, and helps more than 50,000 women in need every year. We also get people volunteering as well as building their own lives, and this sends out ripples of service, and a cycle of giving and receiving that blesses many more lives in turn.

My own sense of mission grew from the pain of my past, and so I'm grateful for those experiences. I am also deeply grateful that I am living my passion. I am grateful for my trials and that I was able to rise above them. I am grateful that I know how to be of service to others. Most of all, I'm grateful that God is always there rooting for all of us, as we work to transform our lives.

Give God the praise every morning as you awaken. Don't check the traffic or wake the children or make the coffee until you turn your thoughts toward heaven. Give God the praise during the day when you notice anything that evokes gratitude, and definitely give God the praise as you go to sleep at night. Fill your mind and heart with all of what you are grateful for as you drift off to sleep and your rest will be blessed with a sense of abundance.

God's time is his own and your prayers will be answered in His time. Just know that holding onto faith and living with gratitude will provide every day miracles and a protective feeling of being surrounded by grace.

A Final Word

WE CAN ALL HOLD A VISION of what it means to experience God's grace and to be blessed with every day miracles. Imagine your life moving forward from this day. See yourself as being full of gratitude and faith. Know that you have the ability to connect with God more often. Trust that you can live an authentic life and that this is exactly what God wants for you. Know that you aren't alone and that your brothers and sisters experience the same difficulties and joys, and that we are all watched over by a loving God.

I encourage you to form an Everyday Grace Everyday Miracle Circle wherever you are in the world. As you gather together, share your stories, pray, read, plan, and eat together. Celebrate the changes you are able to make and give each other the gifts of speaking your truth, of listening, and of cheering each other on in your growth and development.

Together, we can create a better world, one family, neighborhood, city, region, and country at a time. As each of us comes into our larger life, with help from God, we will bless those around us in countless ways. Once we are living our best life we can soften the conflict that surrounds us. We can live abundantly, and we can make sure a child has food in her belly, that the sick are cared for, and that more of our brothers and sisters can experience the life God wants us all to live.

When we are doing well, we are surrounded by God's grace, and even during our darkest times, we are encircled by mercy, and miracles. I encourage you to preserve the story of you life as an inspiration to others. As we share what we have survived and how we have grown we create a testament of how God has worked in our lives. A blank page follows here as a reminder to share your own story. Without your story, this book is not complete.

ACKNOWLEDGEMENTS

THIS BOOK WAS BORN OF MANY EXPERIENCES and has emerged from my travels to many interesting places to meet with wonderful people. It was born out of the sisterhood I felt in a meeting in Singapore when women asked that I be given more speaking time, and I knew that the stories we were sharing were making a difference. Women have reached out to me in New Zealand and Jamaica, and I have spoken at Oxford in the U.K. in an elegant coffee shop. I have taken the ferry to meet with Rev. Gola in Auckland, and made new friends in countless cities and towns. I've met with the minister in an Episcopal church in Cape Cod Massachusetts, and with women in the high desert of Santa Fe, New Mexico. I've stayed with a total stranger who invited me to a costume party and outfitted me from her closet at the last minute. I've shared meals with re-markable people in all these places, and I've heard stories and seen examples of God's grace.

Thank you, God, for the idea of bringing these stories together in the pages of a book so they could be shared. Thanks to my mother Zettie Vernon, who helped me understand that I can do anything, and encouraged me to see that every one of my brothers and sisters in the world can do anything. Thank you to my sister Veronica, who wept when she read the first draft, giving me the cour-age to continue writing. Thanks also for the inspiration of my sister Maxine, who has bravely moved to a new country and is thriving. Thanks for the inspira-tion provided by my brother, the Reverend Wayne Vernon, who answered the call and showed me that I could answer my call as well. Thanks to my sister-in-law Yvonne for her example of how possible it is to always learn and grow. Thanks to my nieces Laurie Ann and Tonie Beth, and my nephews Lamar and Nathan. They bring joy to our family and are such good students that we hold great hope for their futures.

Thanks to Stuart Lyle, who created the beautiful design for this book, as he did with my previous book. And thanks to the Holy Spirit for leading me to Lydia Nibley and Russell Martin, who helped me shape this book. I could never have done it without you two.

I offer prayers of gratitude for all of my friends and family who have helped carry me to the finish line of this project. And thanks to you, dear reader, for going on this journey with me, and with all of the women and men who so generously offered their stories in the pages of this book. Let us all continue to inspire and encourage each other. Praise God!

CONTRIBUTING AUTHORS

Char McCargo Bah, Virginia
Professional Genealogist.
Federal Government Policy Writer.
Chrlb200@aol.com

Sharon Beth Brani, Virginia
Writer. Author.
Licensed Professional Coach
sbrani@ns.gemlink.com
www.sharonbrani.com

Kathy Bruins, Southwest, Michigan
Writer. Elder. Drama Teacher
kbruins@ameritec.net

Dinorah Blackman, Panama
Author
sweetheartdino@yahoo.com
www.lulu.com/blackman

Johnese Burtram, Virginia
Writer. Office Administrator
johnese.burtram@gmail.com

Grace Boneschansker, Canada
Freelance Writer
GrcBon@aol.com

Reverend Dr. Lori Cardona, Florida
Interfaith Minister. Author
loricardona@revlori.com
www.revlori.com

Lucy Cain, Kentucky
Writer. Orthopedic Surgeon's
clinical Assistant
Lucy@allgloryishis.com
www.allgloryishis.com

Lisa Cohen, Florida
Writer. Art Therapist
Lrc4art@yahoo.com

Angalette Dye, Florida
Spoken Word Poet
Substitute Teacher
dangalete@yahoo.com

Minister Mary Edwards, Detroit
Author. Writing Coach.
ministermaryedwards@yahoo.com
www.widowswithwisdom.com

Karen Elengikal, Sidney, Australia
Freelance Writer. Author
www.Godinspired-PhotoArt.com

Peggy Frezon, Rensselaer, New York
Writer. Tutor ESOL
ecritMeg@nycap.rr.com
www.Peggyfrezon.googlepages.com

Anne Fitz Henry, Minnesota
Writer
willqueenroyal@hotmail.com

Pamela K. Hirson, New York
Writer
awriterslife@optonline.net

Mary Haskett, Canada
Writer. Author
mhaskett@rogers.com

Eve Eschner Hogan, Hawaii
Author. Inspirational Speaker.
Writing Coach
EveHogan@aol.com
www.EveHogan.com

Dahlia Walker Huntington
Jamaica and Florida
Writer. Attorney. Event Planner. Radio
Talkshow Power 106FM – Jamaica,
WAVS 1170 AM Florida
JamaicanDawta@aol.com

Susan Karas, Long Island, New York
Freelance Writer
SueZFoofer@aol.com

Karen Reno Knapp, Florida
Freelance Writer
kr4knapp@hotmail.com

Chef Stefano LaCava,
Miami Beach Florida
Chef
chefano007@yahoo.com

Nancy Lucas, Florida
Writer. Business Consultant
NancyLucas@bellsouth.net
www.goin2heavenru.blogspot.com

Catherine Madera, Washington
Author. Ghostwriter
maderam@wwdb.org

Lakisha McClendon, Florida
Spoken Word Poet. Writer
kisha_mcclendon@yahoo.com

Christine Miles, New Zealand
Freelance Writer
christine.miles@xtra.co.nz
www.signofthetimes.org.au

Valora Otis Cottage, Minnesota
Inspirational Writer. Author
otis6@tcq.net

Diane Pitts, Alabama
Author Physical Therapist
danddpitts@earthlink.net

S. Brenton Rolle,
Boynton Beach Florida
Teacher. Trainer. Writer
Brolle14@yahoo.com

Melissa Annette Santiago, Florida
Writer
mellabella635@aol.com

Pachent Gordon – Smythe,
Cayman Islands
Writer Teacher
Pachent@hotmail.com

Chaya Srivatsa, India
Writer. Women Development Consultant.
Trustee Guild of Women Achievers
womenach@hotmail.com
www.womenachievers.com

Lynne Cooper Sitton, Florida
Author. Illustrator. President Broward
County Florida Chapter of American
Christian Writers
LynneCSitton@cs.com

Vera Thomas, Columbia, South Carolina
Writer
vot131@aol.com

Terri Tiffany, Clermont, Florida
Writer
Talker445@yahoo.com

Tonie – Beth Vernon, Jamaica
Student
Tonie-Beth@hotmail.com

Estella Washington, Florida
Writer. Inspirational Speaker
info@givingthekeys.com
www.givingthekeys.com

Karen Ward, Australia
Writer
jkmje@grapevine.net.au

Lora Woodhall, Canada
Writer. Teacher
a_seashell2@yahoo.ca

Dallas Nicole Woodburn,
Ventura California
Writer. Author
dallaswoodburn@aol.com
www.zest.net/writeon

Suzanne Windon, China
Writer. English Teacher
aussiesuzanne@psmail.net

Barbara Williams, Charleston,
North Carolina
Writer Licensed Counselor
bawilms@comcast.net

Debbie Willows, Canada
Writer. Speaker Paralympian
dwillows@sympatico.ca

Nicole Wild, Miami, Florida
Executive Director Chapter 2.
Executive Director Women's Alliance
nicole@thewomensalliance.org
www.chapter2clothing.org

Amy Wiley, Washington
sparrowsflight@peoplepc.com
www.sparrowsflight10.blogspot.com

ADDITIONAL POWER PRODUCTS BY AUTHOR

scriptures for meditation, comfort and daily living

Scriptures for mediation, comfort and daily living.

The is an incredible pocket size book of 100 bible verses. These are the scriptures I used to change my life from a burnt out attorney to now a person who helps people all over the world. Get a copy for yourself or a friend. You can order from us or where ever books are sold.

Book $15.00

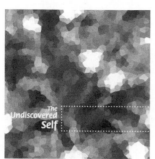

Undiscovered Self CD for Meditation, Relaxation and Stress Reduction.

The Undiscovered Self combines alpha, theta and delta tones to lower your anxiety, stress, improve sleep and heighten your productivity.

CD $13.95

Decision To Change CD

sets out six easy steps to changing your life.

CD $11.50

Lorna Owens is a highly sought after speaker, life coach, and author who travels to speaking engagements and seminars and workshops around the world. She is the host of the Lorna Owens Radio Show, and the founder of Women Behind Bars, an empowerment program for incarcerated women. Lorna also founded the award-wining And the Woman Gather Literary Jazz Brunch, an annual event that supports the work of a charitable foundation, and the Women Travel First Class Retreat, an annual spa and golf retreat that supports women executives and community leaders in their professional and personal growth. Lorna is based in Miami Beach, Florida and also works and plays in her homeland of Jamaica.

For Speaking Engagement, Workshops/Seminars or Life Coaching
Contact Lorna Owens Inc.

20 Island Ave. Ste 903, Miami, Florida 33139
Tel. 305-573-8423, Fax. 305-604-6311
contact@lornaowens.com | www.lornaowens.com